When Dolls are Broken

When Dolls are Broken

Emotional Healing for Women

Angela Bufford Taye

 authorHOUSE®

AuthorHouse™ LLC
1663 Liberty Drive
Bloomington, IN 47403
www.authorhouse.com
Phone: 1-800-839-8640

Published by AuthorHouse   01/24/2014

ISBN: 978-1-4918-4942-2 (sc)
ISBN: 978-1-4918-4941-5 (hc)
ISBN: 978-1-4918-4946-0 (e)

Library of Congress Control Number: 2014900471

Contents

Dedication

This book is dedicated to every woman who has been so hurt, so depressed that she could barely lift up her head. To every woman who has been so broken inside that she thought she was beyond repair. To every woman who ever looked at the circumstances of her life and thought within herself that she just didn't want to continue living. To every woman that desires to be changed.

To every broken doll . . . . Be healed in the name of **Jesus**!

Foreword

It's all here. Honest expression, focused with a serious purpose, and even fearless when Angela audaciously—and bravely—seeks healing, love and self-acceptance. There is no doubt that writing this book was a labor of love. What struck me even more than Angela's quiet strength was her raw honesty? Her heart felt honesty made her writing not only riveting, but relatable, for beneath all the hurt and emotional pain her stories were about real authentic human beings and emotions. It is at this point where you stop and recognize. You realize what the author is sharing with you . . . the most intimate details of her life. You remind yourself-this is not fiction, this is real. This book is about the life of one woman, but shared by many women.

As I read, I found my mind wondering about my life experiences and how God has always walked with me, but I didn't always walk with Him. I found myself wondering why? Why has Angela opened the door for the world to look at such personal and private situations? I can see why she wrote this book. She wants to help people and it is working, she has just helped me . . . a lot. At that moment, my perception of this book changed.

I began to see the lessons and blessings that were jumping off every page. I also began to think of friends who were facing certain obstacles and situations in their lives and how this book would help them. Although Angela's life is about serving God and helping other people, I don't believe she yet realizes that this book is destined to set women free of their emotional pain and scars and allow them to live the lives God intended. Allow God to use these pages to plant your feet on your destiny path.

I bought a copy of *Something More: Excavating your Authentic Self* written by Sarah Ban Breathnach. It is one of the best books about self-evaluation that I have ever come across. *When dolls are broken* by Angela Bufford Taye is the same type of book. It will cause you to look at yourself in ways that are crucial if you want to live a fulfilled Christian life.

As we begin taking this in-depth, honest journey of what we are doing with our lives. We see how everything that happens in our lives is a lesson that prepares us for blessings from God.

Prior to receiving the manuscript, I never knew my niece's level of emotional pain and scars. Although we would talk on occasion and I sensed her pain, I would just pray that she would continue to be strong. Family members would often say we look alike and I smiled inside as I thought maybe I'm not "ugly" after all. I was proud to be associated with someone that is beautiful. Through reading this book and discussing it with her, we have experienced epiphanies that helped us come to terms with the past choices and revelations to our destiny. As you read her book, you will be in awe of God's presence in her life. She has a personal light that shines throughout each chapter. It becomes obvious to the reader that she has integrity; faith and a quiet strength that is quite admirable. When I finished the manuscript and laid it down, I was awed by her honesty, how she has been true to herself. Those famous lines by Shakespeare that he gave us in Hamlet came to mind,

"This above all: to thine own self be true,

And it must follow, as the night the day,

Thou canst not then be false to any man."

Angela has followed Shakespeare's advice and through it she has moved closer to what God wants her to become. I am honored that she asked me to write a foreword to her book. Her words and example have inspired me to become a better me. Dare to begin the journey. These pages hold truths that can change, inspire, and encourage you to have faith and boldly declare that you are worthy of God's love.

Terri McCrary Ed. S, Behavioral Specialist, Life-Coach

Acknowledgements

To God be the Glory! I'm so grateful to my Lord, Savior, King, Friend, Confidant and Counselor, Jesus Christ. I give God all honor and praise for his faithfulness throughout my life—during times when I could sense his presence and the times when I could not. There is no God besides Jehovah, no Savior but Jesus and no comforter like the Holy Spirit!

To my eldest children Cordney and Michael, Oh the times we had when you guys were growing up; some good, some bad and some GREAT! I love you guys so much. Always remember that God, not man, is the author and finisher of your faith and He who began a good work in you will complete it. To my babies Gia and Tia you fascinate me every day. I love you!

To my parents Donnie and Veronica, thanks for all of your help and support! Mama, I don't take it lightly that you cared for the girls and gave me the opportunity to write. Thank you! Grandma Elizabeth thanks for praying for me and being an excellent example of a godly woman.

Florence Flugaur, thanks for your *keen* eye and endless encouragement. Terri McCrary, Dr. Monica Janzen and Dr. Kenneth Walker, I really appreciate you. May the Lord continue to bless you and do good to you!

To Pastors Bobby and Roselle Chiles, you have instilled so much into others and you have spent your lives building up the kingdom of God without compromising or exalting yourself. You deserve double honor! I'm glad to be a product of the Youth Crusade Evangelistic Center Church Family where love abides. I love you all. God continue to bless you and increase your harvest!

Pastor Joe and Diana Glaze and the Pole Branch Baptist Church family . . . I can barely express my gratitude for you and for the love and support you have given us far and near. I love you guys so much and I will always consider PBMBC my home.

Pastor Dr. Josef Howard, I don't think I would have finished this book without your encouragement. I appreciate you and Sis. Lees. Thank you so much for all of your help, encouragement, counseling and support. May God continue to bless you richly!

To Pastor Natt and Margaret Friday and all of the Bethel Robbinsdale Church family; thank you for welcoming me and my family. Thanks for your support and encouragement.

Finally, Carrie L. Cofer, you fixed a lot of things for me, the doll was just one of many. I love and appreciate you!

Preface

When a doll is broken, it's hard to see the beauty and purpose for which it was made. The gift that was meant to be a companion, a comfort during difficult times, a help to overcome fears, a friend, a blessing—now lies tossed aside.

There are women all over the world lying discarded like broken dolls. The only difference is that these women feel the pain of brokenness and desperately want to be made whole and to be looked upon according to the value that the Creator has placed upon them.

I can remember having a beautiful doll that encountered some wear and tear and she ended up needing to be mended. She was what we called an "adoption doll" and she was made to look as close to human as possible in that era. She did nothing special like poop or drink from a bottle, but she was expensive because she was handmade. Therefore, her maker placed a high value on her. I suppose the fact that it took time and thought to make the doll; its designer wanted others to know the carefulness put into making the doll so that she might be treasured and handled according to the value placed upon her. Well, needless to say, not everyone knew how to treasure such dolls. Some were torn by two friends who wouldn't take turns with the doll; others were torn by owners who were careless; while some were even torn by strangers who didn't know or care about the value placed on the doll by its maker. There are even dolls that are placed into the hands of those who do not want them and they are daily abused. The result is a broken and tattered blessing that appears to be a curse. Some like my doll were torn by mistake.

However, I loved my doll, she was valuable to me. I had an aunt whom I stayed with often. She could sew so; I carried my doll to her. She looked at it and she said, "I can fix it." I can't explain the satisfaction and relief that came from that single statement.

Nevertheless, as I've grown and raised children of my own, gone through many difficult times and been in contact with many women who have also done the same, some successfully and others not so well. I am convinced that like dolls, there are many broken and torn women whose purpose and value has been greatly distorted because of the degree of which they've been broken. I'm so glad, elated, overjoyed that we have a Maker who still attributes great value to the work of his hand. In a woman's worst state of brokenness, his response is, "I can fix it."

That's right, your Heavenly Father who fearfully and wonderfully made you, took you from your mother's womb, and sent his son to die for the sins of the world is able to repair every broken woman who comes to Him.

This book contains many personal true stories in order to establish patterns that were set in my life and how some of those same patterns are formed in the lives of other broken women. It is my intent that the reader will see the difference that Jesus can make in a life regardless of its dysfunction. It is not my intent to hurt, offend or blame anyone for my past or present life. I love and respect my parents and I have a good relationship with them. Anything mentioned concerning them during my childhood is only to give the reader an honest vision of the activities of my life at that time. My parents gave their consent before publication. Names, places and events have been altered to protect the identity of the subjects.

Chapter 1

Why?

No one wants to live a broken, subdued, and crushed: fragmented life. This truth does not prevent one out of every eight women in the US from experiencing clinical depression within their lifetime which, often leads to brokenness. Over twelve million women are diagnosed each year, most frequently in ages 25-44. There are numerous medications on the market to treat such illness when they are caused by chemical, biological, genetic, developmental, reproductive or hormonal imbalances. However, in many cases, the cause isn't chemical; it is the result of a life event which caused emotional or physical trauma. Events such as: abortion, sexual abuse, divorce, the death of a loved one or a drastic change in life circumstances.

What do we do when we are experiencing depression caused by events in our lives? One of the first things we do is try to determine why. We want to know why we feel the way we do, think the way we think and behave the way we behave. We want to know why certain events have transpired in our lives. Why things are the way they are. We want to know why we feel broken.

Well, it was easy to establish why my doll was broken. I loved my doll but I didn't realize how fragile she was. Thank God that He not only loves us but He knows how much we can bear. Even the most devout Christian has at some point said, "Lord, why is this happening?" I don't know if the circumstances would change if we received an instant answer to that question. But, when you have been abused or violated; 'why' becomes a plaguing question. Getting past some events seem unattainable without investigating 'the why.' The pain attached to negative memories can cause constant discontent. You feel there must be some explanation. Yet, seeking to find the why in the hurts, pains, ups and downs of a broken life isn't always easy.

We know that our own actions are contributing factors to the kind of life we live, but we cannot control all of the events of life. Those events that we cannot control also play a part in our quality of life and emotional health but, they do not have to dictate the quality of them. During those times when 'the why', of a thing becomes a nag, we look to God for answers.

Only God knows the path we take. He is sovereign and He knows every twist, turn, situation and circumstance that has, is or will be occurring in our lives. He sees our hurts and tears. He knows our fears. He knows where we are, how we got there and why we are there. More importantly, He knows where He is taking us.

God knows how He will bring us to His expected end. He knew the end from the beginning so every choice we make, every choice that was made for us He knows and it doesn't change His desired end for us. Everything that happens in this life is a result of someone's choice. It's the result of choices that we become the people we are. Whether the choices are good, bad or thrust upon us, they shape our lives. You may be thinking; I didn't choose this. I didn't choose to be abandoned, abused, raped, poor, misunderstood, mistreated, scarred, and sick, you name it, and you are right. It is rare that anyone would choose to be a victim of any kind of abuse or hardship. Our lives can be affected by someone else's bad choice just as our choices can affect others. For instance:

A woman we will call Lydia was pregnant. During her pregnancy she smoked, drank alcohol and used marijuana. When her child was born he would randomly shake because of withdrawal symptoms. Many infants who experience withdrawal symptoms after birth later have trouble with memory and paying attention according to the 2011 article, "Dangers of smoking marijuana while pregnant."

The child had not made a choice to do bad or good. Yet, he was affected by his mother's choice. That choice didn't remove God's love for him or His plan for the child's life. Lydia had a Christian family member who would often lay hands on the child and speak life over him. Today he does not exhibit any mental problems; he is an honor roll student who excels on standardized test. Our God is an awesome God!

Then, there are some events that happen solely for the Glory of God. The key is for us to look to glorify God in whatever situation we are in. It may simply be that glorifying Him will direct someone else to Him. It is interesting and somewhat like a mystery that God has so fearfully and wonderfully made us, gave us free will, gave us gifts and talents and then wants us to use those things to be a benefit to others. We can understand that when it comes to good things occurring in our lives, God wants us to share them to be a blessing to others. But, He also wants to use the hurt in our lives to be a blessing to others. Many of the challenges and pains that we experience have little or nothing at all to do with us. It has to do with His glory.

To glorify means to give honor, praise and admiration. There was a man in the bible that was born blind. Jesus healed him. Once his eyes were opened, in the end he worshipped and glorified God (John 9:1-41). That was a good thing but it is easy to worship, praise, and give honor and admiration when we receive or witness an instant miracle. The years he spent living with his blindness were probably not as easy. When he received his sight the people who were present and anybody who knew him could plainly see that he had been touched by the hand of God. What they didn't know is that God knew him before they did and His hand was always upon him to be glorified in his affliction at God's appointed time. If you are thinking, "I live in an ongoing situation that potentially causes pain and even shame. How can God be glorified in this?" Well, God can still get the glory in situations that are not glorious. Here is an example:

As a mother of a child diagnosed with multiple mental and behavioral disorders that were present at birth, I understand your dilemma. Every so often I would just ask, why? I would sit in meeting after meeting; go to doctor after doctor and specialist after specialist answering all kinds of questions that made me feel as if they thought I was somehow responsible for the disability. I prayed and fasted and asked God to heal her. I had others to pray for and with her. The behaviors persisted and we didn't receive an instant manifestation of a miracle. I could not see how God could be glorified by not providing a miracle. I could not see how He was glorified in her pain, in my pain or the shame attached to some of the behaviors. But when we glorify God in the midst of affliction it illustrates God's sustaining power. It is a witness that His strength is made perfect in weakness.

I would not have made it through without Jesus nor would I have been able to experience the peace and joy that I had as we faced daily challenges. It caused others around us to see fruits of the spirit developing in me even when I didn't notice it. To God be the glory.

Now, there will always be someone watching you. Some will not be looking for the Christ in your situation. Many people will look at your condition and make assumptions just as the disciples did when they saw the blind man. They questioned Jesus, "who sinned, the man or his parents that he was born blind?" Jesus replied, "Neither was it this man's sins or his parents that caused him to be blind but that the works of God should be manifest in him" (John9:2-3). It doesn't matter how long a situation persists, when you didn't choose it, and someone else didn't choose it for you—Always assume that your situation is a setup that the work of God may be manifest in **His** time. At that time His work will glorify Him as it always does. In the meantime, you can glorify Him with your words and actions. There are people watching how God is sustaining you in your trial and seeing the fruit being developed in you. Let your light so shine before men that they may see your good works and glorify your Father who is in heaven (Matthew 5:16). When you glorify God it can provoke others to do the same. Setting your focus on these things will reduce the stress of contemplating why.

If we persist and try to assess our situation in hopes of knowing the **'why'** for everything that occurs in life here on earth, we will be tired and disappointed. For some things, regardless of how we seek them, there is no direct answer. There are many things that we will not know at this time or in this life. As Paul said, "For now we see through a dark glass but then face to face: now I know in part but then I will know even as I am known" (I Corinthians 13:12). So, for now, as a young child looks to his parents with trust and admiration we can rest in that same safety in the hands of our Lord Jesus with full assurance of His love and ability. We know that God is capable of handling all the issues of our life, even the ones we don't understand. We can be wholly certain that He has our best interest at heart, knowing that He loves us and He will cause all things to work together for the good of those who love Him and who are the called according to His purpose (Romans 8:28).

In all actuality, knowing why we are where we are *can* change our perspective but, knowing how we've become who we are is what gives us the knowledge we need to invoke change. In order to do that; we must be willing to look back at the facts of our lives.

Chapter 2

Looking back to move forward

When I think back on the repairs made on my doll, it was never really important 'how' she had gotten into the shape she was in. She didn't have thoughts, feelings and emotions. She didn't have responsibilities and obligations to meet that would interfere with her repair. My aunt could fix her regardless of what caused her to be in disrepair. However, it was useful for me to know how she was torn so that I could avoid having the same problem again. Likewise, for a living, breathing, broken woman; God can make the repairs regardless of the cause of disrepair. But, it is important to know how the brokenness came to be; So that as much as it lies within your power, you can avoid a repeat of the same situation. For most women, this will require some examining of the past. For some it may only be a few months or a couple of years and for others like me, it may require looking way back into childhood.

For as long as I can remember, I had to force myself to feel good about myself. I needed to look back and find out where I first began to have feelings of inadequacy and what caused me to feel that way. As I reminisced, some distinct memories came to mind;

> My parents were divorced and like most families who go through divorce, there were many extenuating circumstances. I was very young at the time and I don't remember much about a family life that included both

my parents together. I do remember loving my dad very much and always wanting to see him. I didn't see him very often. That made me sad but in my mind at that time he was the best thing ever. If he said he was coming to visit me, I would want to sit outside until dark waiting for him. I somehow thought that if I just stayed there on the porch he would show up. I had to be made to come in the house on more than one occasion.

He remarried and his new wife had a beautiful daughter who was the same age as me. I think we were about 7 years old because we were in second grade. As an adult, I understand that my parents were young and parenting is not easy, we all make mistakes. But, at the time all I could see and feel was that my dad wasn't there. All I had of him was empty promises. Meanwhile, my step sister and I attended the same school and we were enrolled in the same class. Therefore, I had the opportunity to see her on a daily basis during the school year and I was aware every time she got something new. During that time period, the early eighties, for a second grader, getting anything from your parents meant a lot. So, more importantly, I knew that I *wasn't* getting anything. I couldn't understand why he didn't think of me. This was the beginning of the feelings of inadequacy, rejection and just plain feeling unwanted. Although, my dad came for me three or four times, I always felt like my step sister's guest rather than my Dad's daughter. After all, it was her home, her mom in the kitchen and when she said 'daddy' it sounded a lot more natural than I felt saying it to someone I saw occasionally. I felt very out of place and unsure of myself even at that young age. I used to look at her at school and wonder why he seemed to care for her and not me. I was only 7 years old but his presence in her life said love while the lack thereof in my life screamed rejection. Like most children, I never said anything, I just internalized it and I would imagine doing something good and making my daddy proud. As time passed, the love and desire I had to please my Father began to turn into anger and withdrawal from him. This isn't uncommon for children of divorce. 1.5 million American children each year have parents who divorce. According to Judy Wallenstein, in 'The Unexpected Legacy of Divorce: a 25 year land mark study,' most children of divorce experience depression. Twenty five percent of those children will experience serious social, emotional or psychological troubles as adults. I guess I was one of those twenty five percent.

There was one event that rekindled my hope but only to put the flames out again. At age eleven, my stepmother dropped off a Christmas present to me from my dad. It was a white blouse and a pink jean skirt with white pinstripes and I was glad to get it. This was only the second gift I'd received from him in my life at the time and that day was a complete surprise. I was so happy. As I think of the smile on my face when I held that box, it brings tears to my eyes because it meant more to me than the contents. For that moment, I felt that I wasn't forgotten and that feeling lasted several days. When I saw my family members during the holidays, I wore the outfit and I told anybody who would listen that my dad had given it to me.

Right after New Year's Day, school resumed. So, what did I wear my first day back to school after the holidays? That's right, the white blouse and pink and white pin striped skirt. It would also be my attire for winter pictures with the addition of a navy blue sweater. Unfortunately, this was the end of my great joy surrounding that gift.

When I reached my classroom, my stepsister gave me her lengthy list of gifts including a desk top computer which was very expensive during that time. I felt ashamed and hurt, not to mention angry. I was also jealous and secretly I resented my stepsister and the fact that my dad was so concerned about her education and had not given me one tool, not even a pencil and paper to assist in my education. I even resented the rules he had for her such as making sure that she read for at least an hour every day. I think it bothered me that he cared enough to try to give structure to her life while I never had to answer to him about anything. It seemed that he didn't care enough to set any boundaries for me nor did he even know what was going on in my life. I resented that she had what I wanted more than anything, two parents. So, after that, I didn't ask to go visit him and he didn't bother to ask me to come visit him. Many people told me that I was like my daddy or that I looked like my aunt and I liked that because although I didn't know her very well, I thought she was pretty and I knew she was very smart. I tried to focus on that. As far as my relationship with my dad, by age twelve our relationship was really nonexistent and I basically just tried not to think about it. At the time, I didn't know I was about to enter a period of my life where I needed my dad the most. I don't know which was worst, feeling rejected or so desperately wanting to be accepted by the person I felt rejected by.

Nevertheless, this was the beginning of my 'how.' This was the basis upon which my thoughts concerning myself were established. Now, looking back on this issue did not change anything but it did lead me to the root cause of many insecurities that later manifested themselves in my life. It gave an explanation for my natural way of thinking and it allowed me to identify how depression, rejection and the fear of it entered my life. Many young girls and women suffer because of rejection. The good news is that we have a Savior who can relate to our emotional distress. Isaiah 53:3 says,

"He was despised and rejected of men; a man of sorrows and acquainted with grief: and we hid as it were our faces from Him; He was despised and we esteemed Him not." Verse 4 goes on to say, *"Surely He has born our grief and carried our sorrows: yet we did esteem Him stricken and smitten of God and afflicted."*

Have you ever felt this way? Have you ever felt smitten of God and had circumstances that you felt supported those feelings? Being rejected by a love one whether it is a parent, spouse, child, sibling or a friend can surely cause a person to feel that God Himself also rejects them. It is a deep hurt that feels like punishment. But, you can rest assured that if you go to God, He will never reject you. Jesus says, "All that the Father gives me will come to me and he that comes to me; I will in no wise cast out" (John 6:37). You can give your grief and sorrows to God; His Son has already taken punishment for us and given us the right to exchange our sorrows for joy. God is able to take your pain and my pain and use it to be a healing balm for others as He did with Jesus. Jesus was wounded for our transgressions; He was bruised for our iniquities: the chastisement of our peace was upon Him; and with His stripes we are healed (Isaiah 53:5). His pain produced healing for the whole world. If we allow God to do so, He will take our pain, repair us and send us out to recommend His craftsmanship to others who are in need of repair. Some people who seem to be random in your life are there for a purpose as you are also strategically placed in the lives of others. For example :

A beautiful Christian woman entered my life for a brief encounter or at least so it seemed at the time. I was 12 years old and I didn't know she would make a world of difference in my life. Her name is Kay Finnell. My father and his family moved and my mother had allowed me to try out for the junior cheer squad. I practiced and practiced at home and on the day of tryouts while I waited for my number to be called I kept telling myself that I would do exactly what I'd been doing at home and I would just pretend that nobody else was there. Well, I did just that but I was so nervous that I misspelled a word and my heart throbbed. I wanted to just stop and leave but I didn't, I kept smiling and I kept going. To my surprise, I made the squad. They only chose eight girls. One of the judges, Kay Finnell, was also an English teacher. She spoke with me later and she said it was really hard to choose only eight girls. I said, "I thought I wasn't going to make it especially after I misspelled the word." She replied, "We caught that but that was the reason we chose you. Sometimes things like that will happen and mistakes will occur. We saw that you continued with the same enthusiasm and that was the deciding factor." This was a major boost to my confidence. Boy, did I need confidence. This was my first personal interaction with Mrs. Finnell but not my last.

I had so many things, secret things hidden inside of me. Things that I always felt were my fault and my doing somehow. It still scares me now that people are so trusting of friends and family members with their children. It is a common assumption that children are safe with people that are well known by their parents. Yet, over 300,000 children each year are reported as victims of sexual molestation and 30% of these atrocities are committed by family members. In the aftermath of such things, mothers are often ridiculed for not suspecting, knowing or acting. Sometimes, secrets peek out but we would just rather not see them. However, many times the mother has had her own terrible issues in that area that she is trying to live with while raising children and pretending it never happened. It is reported that 1 in 4 women in the US have been molested before the age of 18.

A broken doll can hardly mend another if she hasn't been mended. Nevertheless, I still cringe at gatherings when I see men interacting with young female children and I watch them closely.

I can remember the day that I turned thirteen. I felt some sense of boldness that I hadn't had before. I remember telling myself that from now on nobody is going to touch me again and make me feel dirty because this time I would stand up to them myself. I don't know if they saw boldness about me or thought that I would tell now that I was older because it stopped. I was relieved. I really didn't want to tell anyone that I had been touched inappropriately because I was ashamed; I just wanted it to stop. Yet, I was prepared to tell if I had to. The relief didn't last long. Statistics say that girls who have a prior history of molestation have a 1000% chance of reoccurring. I was about to become a factor in those statistics. I would soon experience what would set the tone of the remainder of my teenage years and the next several years of my life thereafter.

The following month, after turning thirteen, my bold declaration fell to the ground. It was summer time and on this particular day my mother asked a friend of hers to allow me and my friend to stay at her house until she got off from work. The day passed without incidence until we three went to the Laundromat. Our caretaker for the day helped us to start the wash for the machines but said she had to go home for something and she would be back. She gave us coins for the dryer and said to put the clothes in the dryer if the wash stopped before she got back.

The clothes washed and dried and we folded them, still no sign of our caretaker for the day.

We sat and waited. Soon, her adult step son showed up and said she sent him to pick us up. The three of us loaded the clothes into the vehicle and went back to the house. We were each carrying baskets into the house but I didn't see the caretaker.

When I took my basket into the back room, the step son came in behind me with a basket and shut the door and locked it. I started screaming and telling him to let me out and calling for my friend who hurried to the door and she began to hit it and scream for him to let me out. He did not. He wrestled me to the floor and eventually took what little of myself I had left. Sweat and tears ran down my face and blood ran down my legs from the pastel plaid shorts that were still intact. Although I had been violated, never had anyone gone so far as intercourse . . . as far as rape. I had no idea why I was bleeding; I didn't know what happens when virginity was lost. I really knew nothing about the actual act of sex until that moment and what I learned was that it was terribly painful.

As soon as he released me, my friend and I left walking to my house. She explained it in these words, "He popped your cherry." She then went on to tell me some of her own personal information. We were both only 13 at the time so her words and logic made me *feel* better. I was still confused and uncomfortable but somehow after our conversation, I *felt* more like I'd entered into womanhood and less like a victim. I didn't want to be a victim. She behaved as if what happened was a normal everyday thing. In most cases, children who are sexually abused repeatedly, sadly start to accept it as a part of life. I look back at that day as the day that set the tone for the next several years of my life. I was just barely a teenager but I had been exposed to things that I shouldn't even know about.

After that came one bad decision after another. My violator called afterwards because he wanted to be sure I didn't tell. He stated that he was calling to see if I was ok and then he added that he hadn't done anything to me and wanted to know why I was crying. He pretended that he liked me. I believed him because I wanted to be liked; I wanted to be loved even though I didn't know what love was. He would from that time tell me to come to one place or another and I would go. Other adults would be home and they said nothing so I began to think that there was nothing wrong with it like he said.

Four months after my thirteenth birthday, I was pregnant. That's when I found out that he was not driven by deep feelings for me that day in August. That was just a cover up for the wrong act that had been performed. First, came the name calling and denial that he had ever touched me. Then, the accusations came that it was me, a thirteen year old, had forced myself on him. My mother was deeply hurt and she confronted him. This made me angry because I was already ashamed and I just wanted everything to go away. I never discussed what happened from the beginning with my family because I didn't think anyone would believe me. I felt broken and worthless. Finally, he made an offer to pay for an abortion.

His behavior towards me at that time sparked the same emotion that I get now when I read or listen to the biblical account of what happened between King David's children Amnon and Tamar in II Samuel Chapter 13. Amnon and Tamar had different mothers but they were siblings. Amnon was moved by lust to the point that he raped his sister even after she pleaded with him not to commit such a foolish act. You see, Amnon didn't consider that he was about to cause a precious doll to be broken. He didn't consider that she could be affected by his choice for the remainder of her life. Amnon followed his desire and when he was finished with Tamar, the bible says that he hated her and had her put out of the room and away from him. After he had gratified himself, the guilt was so overwhelming he didn't even want to look at her. Tamar lived in desolation with her other brother Absalom for the remainder of her life. She never received the healing she needed to be released from the guilt and shame brought on by Amnon's act of foolishness. Consequently, Amnon did not live to witness his sister's long term pain because Absalom eventually killed him because of what he had done to their sister. What a sad story with a sad outcome that could have been avoided.

Men, if you realize there is a perversion or evil desire lurking in your flesh, seek help. God loves you and even if you have already acted on your undesirable inclinations, He wants to help you. Jesus died for you too! For your sake and for the sake of your potential victim(s), think twice before you cause any doll to be in disrepair due to any form of abuse, violence or negligence. Allow God to make you whole in order that you may not go about causing brokenness and pain. God has given the man a great responsibility as the head of woman. He has given you the ability to be a leader and protector. Think about that before you make a decision to harm the very ones you have been given the mandate to protect. The choice you make could mean life or death. At the very least, it will be life altering to you and your victim. My life was definitely altered.

That event triggered many years of depression and halfhearted attempts of suicide, bad decisions, aimless promiscuity between the ages of 14 and 15 and a premature marriage at the age of 20 that didn't last a year. Children that are sexually abused are at a higher risk for risky sexual behavior, depression, substance abuse, criminal behavior, destructive tendencies and even suicide. When your own actions are bad, you may begin to reckon whether your violators were all that wrong. It is common for sexually abused children to be made to feel guilty by their perpetrator(s). Often times our society doesn't help with that because children are often blamed for their own abuse. The feelings of guilt began to grow in me as a child and they still thrived for many years as an adult.

Thank God that He has a way of bringing truth to the surface.

Since that time, I've had three different people confess to me that this person did the same thing to them and they didn't know my story. In one of the cases, the girl was able to get away. Thank God for that! I learned of this during my latter teen years. I was taking a science course and a female student pulled me aside and inquired about my daughter. She went on to say that my daughter's dad tried to sexually attack her cousin but she got away. She gave some strikingly familiar details concerning the struggle and his method of attempted overpowering. Her account was so familiar, I didn't have to visualize it; I'd lived it.

The third and most recent case was eighteen or nineteen years after what happened to me. I had a client in my beauty salon approach me in the same way as my science classmate. She began inquiring about my daughter. She asked, "Does she ever see her dad?" At this time, my daughter was about 17 or 18 years old. I responded, "No." she goes on to say, "Maybe that's good." Again, where I lived, I was just the girl who was pregnant at 13; no one knew all that happened. She didn't know my story.

This young lady was known in the community and she used to get in trouble a lot. As I listened to her, I hurt for her especially when she said, "I didn't do anything because I've been in so much trouble that nobody would believe me." Many perpetrators never receive punishment or get the help they need in this life because of this. He has never been charged, convicted or even publically accused of anything pertaining to rape or molestation. I was not happy at all to be told what happened with the other girls but it did let me know that I wasn't alone and it dispelled the accusations in my mind that it was somehow my fault.

Nevertheless, when I gave birth to a beautiful baby girl in August of 1988, as she grew she began to exhibit some abnormal behaviors. Her speech was delayed, she had trouble with cognitive skills, and her behavior was irrational. I didn't know what these things meant, I was only 14. They began to run test on her.

She started a pre-kindergarten program at the age of 4, the school term following my high school graduation. More tests were taken. She was soon labeled as being mentally handicapped and I was told that she would not get past the intellectual level of that of a first or second grader. She was sent to counselors, neurologists, and psychologists only to continue to be diagnosed at the age of 7, with additional problems such ADHD and Disruptive Behavior Disorder in addition to the moderately mental disability she had been previously diagnosed of. Outwardly, when she wasn't misbehaving in some way, you couldn't tell that there were any underlining problems and this was frustrating. She had no outward physical deformity so, people would see us and just think she was a 'bad' child who was not being disciplined or cared for. I had people tell me she was just spoiled and I should make her sit down and I should make her behave. People generally pity parents who have children with a physical disability because the problem can be seen. When a child has a psychological or behavioral problem— an internal problem, the parent is often looked upon as a poor parent. Some people even had the audacity to insinuate and even suggest that perhaps this was punishment. I often felt ashamed. I thank God that my mom and my siblings helped me as best as they could during my teen years. But if it hadn't been for Kay Finnell who voluntarily drove to our home multiple times during the week to bring and receive my classwork and give me tests while I was out of school for six weeks, I would not have graduated high school on time and perhaps not at all. I gave birth during the first week of my freshmen year of high school and she made sure I didn't get behind.

My mom's help had given me the chance to go to my high school proms, finish school and begin technical training. Although, my mom and I didn't have a close relationship, I don't know what I would've done without her. My oldest brother always tried to protect me whenever he could and he became a father figure to my daughter. I'm so grateful to God for His grace and mercy.

The only purpose that remembering our past can serve is to deal with and allow God to deal with issues we have left unresolved and then we can give glory to God for the great things He has done. Looking back can be painful but it can serve as a way of recognizing the root of present psychological and emotional troubles. This step is very important.

Many women who have become new creations through Christ Jesus have lived troubled emotional lives because they are bombarded with feelings of guilt and shame. They are not aware of why they are constantly feeling that something is wrong with them. The problem most often is the negative issues and influences that shaped the mind before accepting Christ and learning to see themselves through God's eyes. Those issues have to be dealt with even though salvation has been received and you have a brand new spirit, the mind must be renewed.

The only way to renew the mind or rather, change the way you think into God's way of thinking, is through His word. It is not possible to see yourself **AS** God sees you without knowing **HOW** He sees you. It is only then that you can move forward and glorify God by forgetting; not thinking about or brooding over those things which are behind us and pressing towards the mark of the high call of God which is in Christ Jesus as you walk in the newness of life.

Chapter 3

Brand New

When I first received my doll she was brand new. Everything about her was beautiful. It's always exciting to receive something new. I was very excited when I got my doll. She was in perfect condition. There was nothing broken about her and nothing missing. She was just as her maker had fashioned her. She was flawless.

That excitement, however, was pale in comparison to actually becoming new. Here is what happened on the day that **I** became new:

In May 1997, as I lay on my cousin's bed on a Saturday morning, I was oblivious to the fact that I was on the verge of a conversion that would last a lifetime. That morning, I was supposed to be at work but depression had taken such hold of me that I just lay there crying. I had stayed out all night Friday with a male friend whom I had a fight with. The fight was like the final straw to all of the problems in my life. That night, I cut my wrist. I was so distraught, so tired. I just wanted to rest. I wanted to sleep . . . continuously. I was sick of my life. As I lay there with my eyes closed and tears running down my face, I felt that my only solace would be an indefinite sleep.

I knew that those were not good thoughts. I had been raised going to church. I had been baptized at age 11. I went with my grandmother to church and Sunday school most of the time. After graduating from high school, I only went periodically. But, I still had a strong consciousness of right and wrong. I had a will to do what was right but my decisions didn't reflect it. I knew that I needed to be changed; I knew that I needed God.

So, I talked to God. Later I realized that, that was prayer. I was accustomed to hearing prayer formally and saying childhood prayers but this was just a heartfelt conversation. The last thing I said was, "God take my life and do whatever you want to do with it." I can tell you I felt a peace and calming come over me that I'd never felt before. Every circumstance in my life was unchanged but somehow I felt that all was well. I didn't understand salvation as I do now but at that moment I knew that I was changed. I felt clean, peaceful. I felt brand new!

That is what happens when we accept the word of God, believe that Jesus, the only begotten Son came, lived a sinless life and then died or rather laid down his life for the sins of the whole world. Three days later, God raised him up from the dead with all power in his hand. Instantly, we are no longer simply fleshly beings created by God. We are then spiritual beings. Paul says it best, "Therefore, if any man is in Christ, he is a new creature, and old things are passed away behold all things become new (II Corinthians 5:17)." At that very moment you are translated from being a creation of God to being His very own son/daughter. We actually become God's heirs and joint heirs with Christ. Wow!

It gets even better because it's not based upon our performance or whether the good we've done outweighs the bad. It is not based upon someone else's opinion of you or whether you were considered to be a good person or bad person. It has nothing to do with the station of life you were born into or your present condition. This gift, this change is received solely by the grace of God through faith. According to Romans 10:9 in order to be saved from the wrath that is to come upon the earth you must believe in your heart the Lord Jesus and confess with your mouth that God has raised Him from the dead. It pleased God to do it this way and not according to a merit based system. It is generally the guilt of man that drives us to believe that it mustn't be this simple, especially when we see the brokenness of our lives. It is hard to comprehend that God accepts us 'as is' but, He does. It is the awareness of the reality of God and His holiness that we behold how far we are from Him and His ways. We oftentimes feel the need to try to earn the right to do what He actually made man to do, worship Him. This can be a very frustrating and tiresome process especially once we realize what God already knows, that we cannot overcome sin or the flesh on our own. Glory be to God that He sent His son to do what we could not and He didn't stop there. Our Lord, our sweet Jesus became sin for us. This means that after He lived a life without sin, thus fulfilling the law, He then gave us all of the privileges that He earned: righteousness, eternal life, healing, and access to the Father, the indwelling presence of the Holy Spirit, joy, peace and the forgiveness of sin. We didn't earn any of the privileges that Christ's death, burial and resurrection has allowed us but, they are no less ours because we have lawfully received them. He came, lived and died as a mortal man that we might receive immortal life through Him.

I shared with you my experience, but everyone who comes to Christ has his or her own personal experience. Nevertheless, after receiving this precious gift, we still have real life issues that must be addressed. If we continue to address the issues of life with the same mindset we operated with before becoming new creatures, we are likely to get the same results.

Prior to this, a broken woman normally behaves and develops habits according to the way she thinks and those thoughts more than likely have been established by the events of her life. In the midst of receiving newness of life, negative thoughts, habits, emotional wounds and scars must be healed and new thoughts established in order to see a true outward reflection of inner newness. It is important to keep contact with God through prayer and to read the Bible as well as attend a good Bible study. Depending upon the degree of brokenness a woman has encountered, she may still have trouble coping. At this point, it is wise to seek help.

Chapter 4

Seeking Help

The most important thing about getting help when you need it, is finding out where to go in order to get the kind of help you need.

I didn't know right off where to go to get the proper help for my doll. When I discovered that her arm was ripped, that she was broken, I tried to fix it myself. That didn't go well. I had no idea what to do. Then, I asked another family member for help. She couldn't sew but, she helped me adjust the doll by putting safety pins in it to keep the arm attached. That was a short term remedy but I needed someone who was skilled at sewing. The doll was not fixed. The make shift repair given by my family member caused her appearance to become worse. The safety pins used for the repair only drew more attention to her broken condition.

That's what happens to many broken women who go to the wrong place for help. A broken woman doesn't need to be patched up, she needs to be healed. A person with good intentions who isn't equipped to help may inadvertently cause further harm rather than healing. It can be harmful for a broken woman to look to someone for help who isn't sympathetic to her pain or who is supportive of her wrong behaviors. A broken woman doesn't need to be exploited or justified in wrong actions. She doesn't need a short term remedy for emotional problems that can be life-long. A broken woman needs the kind of help that will last. In most cases, this kind of help must be *sought* after.

It's important to seek help from the Master first. God has no hidden motive for helping you. Love and compassion are His motivation. There are people in the world who take advantage of the hurt, pain and weaknesses of others. God isn't like that. He never misdiagnoses anyone. He does not condemn us nor does He condone wrongdoing. He doesn't hand out prescriptions that are not needed or give bogus counsel in order to get financial gain. God actually cares about you and your emotional health.

God is able to help us supernaturally but oftentimes; He leads us to people who are able to help us. You may be thinking, "How does God lead us?" Well, God still speaks to us today. You may not hear His audible voice saying, "go here" or "do that." But, we have confidence in His word: that as we trust in Him with all our hearts and lean not unto our own understanding and acknowledge Him in all our ways, He will direct our paths (Proverbs 3:5-6). One of the ways that God speaks to us is through His word. He also speaks through others.

There are times when we must have human assistance. During those times we definitely want God to direct us to the right person at the right time, to the one who is able to help us and meet our particular need. God has given us skilled physicians, psychologists, and Christian counselors that are willing and able to help. However, we are not to consult soothsayers, witches, wizards or any form of witchcraft for help, relief, success or anything for that matter. This is idolatry, it is dangerous and an abomination to God

(Deuteronomy18:10-12). This includes psychics, mediums and so called spiritual guides.

In the book of Isaiah, after the children of Israel had turned away from the God who had so graciously delivered them and started to look to other gods to bless them, Isaiah likened them to leaving a fountain, a living well which is plenteous to try to drink from a dry and broken cistern.

This concept of leaving an all-powerful and all loving God to worship another human being as god or to worship something that was created by a human being such as a molten image seems senseless when we read about it. The children of Israel chose to seek help from images made by the hands of a man rather than seeking God.

During those days, wells were very important for water supply for people, animals and crops. So, Isaiah used an analogy likening God to a living well; plenteous and sustaining. He likened any molten image, false god or person or thing that the children of Israel may look to for help as a dry and broken cistern which is not productive in any way.

This is the very thing that occurs when we look outside of God and his ways to find fulfillment and satisfaction. God alone is the mender of broken hearts. The attempt to overcome brokenness by consulting workers of darkness, developing ungodly relationships, or cultivating addictions will only result in more brokenness. God, the living well, is all sufficient and able to quench all who thirst. The thing about empty wells, which are every false god or thing that we look to as God, is that they can never quench the thirst of man. Any time we spend waiting at a waterless well to produce will only increase thirst and weariness. Every broken woman must look to the hills from whence comes our help; all of our help comes from the Lord (Psalms 121:1).

As a woman who was desperately in need of help, I can testify to the words of the Psalmist (94:17), **unless the LORD had been my help, my soul had almost dwelt in silence.**

My soul was truly on the brink of dwelling in silence. At the age of 13 and again at 22, I attempted to take my own life; first by taking pills and secondly by cutting my wrist. The scar is a constant reminder that no matter how hopeless a situation may seem or how bad I feel, God is able to mend whatever is broken in my life because He's done it before.

I spent many years being defeated by depression and its side effects. At that time, in the community that I lived in, it was kind of taboo to display or admit to any kind of emotional, mental or psychological problem. You would be considered to be 'off' or crazy. I didn't want to be labeled as either of those. It was bad enough to live with the thoughts that something must be wrong with me. I didn't need false labels to increase the depression. So, I just held it in until a few years after I became a Christian.

At that time, I received some much needed help from a Counselor who was also a Christian. She was a psychologist and her remedy for me was simply the word of God—it worked! I only had a couple of sessions with her but I still use the same prescription. Just having her to listen constructively to me made an immediate difference. I still feel the onset of depression from time to time but I'm not defeated by it. I use the word of God to chase negative thoughts and emotions away. Today, I have more joy than I've ever had in my life, even during tedious times. My life is far from perfect or even ideal but I'm grateful to God for His goodness, the power of His word and the fact that He has made us and given us the ability to help one another.

So, it seems simple: God is the living well, He is our help and He is sufficient and well able to overcome any obstacles in our lives. What He does not do miraculously, He has given us the gifts, talents and ability to extend help to each other. All we need to do is choose him, serve him and *VOILA*, a storybook happy ending.

But it's not so simple. We will still encounter obstacles in this life. Becoming a Christian or disciple of Jesus Christ doesn't automatically remove all of life's hardships. The difference is that we now have a Father who is able to help and deliver us if we have faith in him. So, where then does the problem arise? The problem arises not at the fact of God's abilities. It is a general belief among Christians that God is able. In fact, He is omnipotent. The problem arises at the question of His willingness.

During hardships it is easy to question God's motives towards us. We don't always understand His method of doing things so we can become doubtful about whether He hears our prayers or if He will answer them. We often allow our circumstances or unmet desires to cause our faith to become obscure. When Satan attempted to deceive Eve, He never tried to convince Eve that God was not real nor did Satan challenge God's ability, authority or right to impose His guideline for Adam and Eve. No, Satan's tactic was much more subtle. He wanted to cause Eve to be unsure about what God actually said and what He meant by it. Satan's intent was to bring confusion concerning God's motives for His instructions. Those tactics have not changed and that's why it is so important that we know God's word and let it be the truth in our lives, above every thought or suggestion. Even today, many people still take the same route of disobedience as Eve, for the same reason: unbelief in God's good intentions towards us. Many times we are disobedient to God's word because we are unsure if the outcome will be what we desire if we do things God's way. It is in His word that we find His will so that as we walk by faith we can also wait patiently knowing that God is both willing and able to bless us. It is His desire to bless us. We can stand firm knowing that God does not want to keep any good thing from those who walk upright before Him. Eve was deceived into believing that her obedience to God would cause her to be disadvantaged. Satan told her that the fruit in the midst of the garden that God had forbidden them to eat would make her wise and she would be like God.

God forbad them to eat the fruit to protect them from the consequences; He was not trying to deny them anything good as Satan was suggesting. Eve chose to look to what God had forbidden to receive what God could freely give her; wisdom. She chose to leave the living well of God's provision to drink from the empty well of Satan's deception.

Needless to say, that empty well brought forth detestable results for all of mankind. Not only did she not receive the wisdom she wanted but she lost what she had: fellowship with God, labor free—comfort in the garden, pain free child birth and life without death. All the while, the very thing she wanted, God could then and can now readily supply. This truth alone can prevent or bring to a halt the digging of empty cisterns and wasting away at waterless wells. It is a comfort and reassurance to know that God will keep His word and He will keep it to YOU!

Let today be the day you dust yourself off and walk away from your place of dryness and drink from the fountain that will cause you to never thirst again and let the peace of God flow through you like a river and water those around you. (For out of your belly shall flow rivers of living water.)All the help you need is available to you. You only need to seek it.

As a child when I sought the right help, from the right place for my doll which, had been broken, I received a solution. My aunt was capable of repairing the doll and she agreed to do so. My doll was going to be repaired! All I had to do was hold on and wait.

Chapter 5

Holding on

When I gave my aunt the doll, I thought she was going to fix it quickly—perhaps in one day—and give the doll back to me. But, she couldn't. She told me that it would take a bit of work. She said she had to take the arm completely off and repair the bodice before putting the arm back again. She also informed me that this meant she had to take her sewing machine out and set it up for that particular type of sewing. Finally, she said she would get it back to me by the weekend. I was disappointed but I had to just hold on and wait.

Not very many people enjoy waiting especially, during the "high tech;" "get it now era" we live in. But when it comes to God and His plan for your unfolding life, there will be times when you must wait. Someone once said, "God may not come when you want Him but He's always on time." This statement implies that though God may not seem to act on our behalf (show up) when *we feel* we need Him most, He **will** act on our behalf (show up) and when He does, it's not a moment too late. While we wait, we must also hold onto God's word and our faith.

As a Christian woman, I can remember slipping back into the depression and suicidal thoughts that I thought were far behind me. I couldn't understand why my life seemed to be a constant public shame. It had been shameful to be pregnant at the age of 13. It had been shameful being a teenage mom and having people stare at your child's unconventional behaviors in public. It was shameful to be 19 years old, unmarried with two children. It was shameful to get married and be separated before the year was over. It was publically shameful to be divorced. It was a shame to be known for the bad things I had done and have nobody know the bad things that had been done to me.

I told myself that maybe I was cursed as some people were saying. Maybe it was because of the sinful life I had lived prior to becoming a Christian. This thought would only enrage me because I knew I was not the only person in the world who was guilty of sin. I knew people who cared nothing for God but they seemed to live happy and prosperous lives. I became conflicted about the love and forgiveness that I'd received from God and the reality of the pains in my life. I had Jesus, and I was certain of that. I still felt that my responsibilities were more than I could handle. There were times when the best I could do was just hold on. Hold on to faith in God and His word. Hold on to gratefulness for His goodness, although nothing looked or felt good.

After receiving Christ, I experienced a peace that I'd never in my life had before and it was so good. As time passed and the years went by and some prayers still seemed unanswered, confusion tried to set in. I was self-employed and I earned enough money to support myself and my children but the most important desire I had in my life at that time was to see changes in my family. I desperately wanted God to heal my daughter. I saw no manifestation of my daughter's mental, psychological and emotional healing although, I'd prayed and prayed and prayed; fasted and prayed some more. So many times I felt tired and overwhelmed but then God strengthened me and I would go on. But, every time it seemed as if things were about to get better, every time something good would happen, things would fall flat again.

At the age of 25, I got engaged to a wonderful, godly man who is also a Pastor. He changed his mind about marrying me or maybe God changed it, I don't know. He eventually married a beautiful Christian woman and they are fulfilling God's will for their lives.

All I know is that even though I was no stranger to being rejected, this was far past anything from my childhood or adulthood for that matter. I felt that it was the grace of God that had brought the Pastor into my life so when things did not work out, I felt as if God Himself had rejected me. I was born again and eternal life was inside of me but I began to feel that I wasn't good enough, just as I had as a child. I even began to think that other people who knew us didn't think that I was good enough. No one ever said to me, "you are not good enough." I had begun to project my inner thoughts about myself onto others. However, I could manage to press on through the thoughts and opinions of others whether they were real or imagined. But, to think that God who knows and sees me always had rejected me was more than I could bear. Of course, God knew my weaknesses, my failures and my shortcomings, but I knew He also knew what no one else could see. God knew how desperate I was for Him. He knew the labors of love that none could see. God saw the prayer, the intercession, the fasting for others. He knew the level of my sincerity even if someone else could doubt it. Nevertheless, God's grace was sufficient and eventually, that disappointment passed but it left a fracture in my confidence towards God and in my assurance of His love for me. Somehow, the unconditional love that I felt from him two years earlier when I received salvation started to feel like every other relationship I'd ever had in my life. I started to feel that with God, if I wasn't good enough, He would leave too or maybe that He never loved me. I allowed my pain to allow me to accept thoughts of doubt concerning God and His will for me. I felt as if God was against me.

A broken woman can start to determine any situation as a negative and feel that the whole world is against her, including God!

During this whole ordeal, in my private conversations with God I would say, "I'm not telling anybody else about you." Soon afterwards, somebody would come along and share a problem with me and I would try and even say within myself that I would not respond. But, somehow His word would come and I could no longer forbear to keep it in. Later that day when I got home, I would cry and ask God, "Why don't you love me, why won't you help me, why won't you heal my daughter or why won't you send someone to help me, why won't you send someone to love me?" I tried to reach out and help others but I always felt that no one cared for me. From my view point, at that time, my life didn't appear to be that of one of God's beloved.

All in all, I didn't want to live my life any other way. I wanted to follow God and I didn't want to go back to the way I was before. I started to rebuke the negative thoughts that came to my mind and finally one day I spoke back to them. I can remember saying out loud . . . even if God doesn't love me; I will still serve him. Although I still had not completely shaken the feelings of rejection and abandonment, I had fully made a decision to continue on the narrow road that leads to eternal life regardless of what I was feeling. I didn't know where my life was headed but I knew I wanted to continue heading towards Jesus. I just wanted to hold on. That was the most I could do at that moment. During that time, I found that God's grace was sufficient for me. I found out that trust in God must not only apply when we like what He's doing or when what He is doing is within our range understanding.

We must trust God even during times when things don't turn out the way we think or the outcome doesn't seem to be in our favor. Our trust in Him must be complete, not only trusting Him to do what we ask but trusting that His will for us is better than our own. We must know that He is aware of the timetables of our life but we must also realize that He isn't confined by them. So, when God has not moved when, where or how we hoped, believed or thought that He would, even though we have made requests that are in alignment with His word, we must know that there is some divine purpose even if we can't see or imagine what it could be. Trust only becomes trust when there is space between having faith and receiving. There is a difference in believing God and trusting Him. Abraham believed God and it was accounted to him as righteousness. Many times we 'believe' God will heal, He will turn things around or come through for us. Nevertheless, we don't trust Him to do it and we seek out other means to accomplish what we have requested of Him. The Lord knows I have been guilty of this and all the while, I felt that I was trusting in God simply because I believed Him. It turned out on more than one occasion; I missed His great intention for me by working the matter out on my own after I felt I had waited enough. Can you imagine the frustration of praying and waiting for something for a considerable amount of time and then deciding to just take matters into your own hand only to find yourself out of the right position to receive what God had prepared for you which was far better? I can tell you it was devastating.

In any case, when you feel that you can't go on, you can't take it any more . . . **Hold On** and keep **Holding On**! Don't be moved by what's going on around you. If everybody at your church is being blessed, if all your friends are rejoicing and you feel that God has forgotten you, don't allow what you think and what you feel to cause you to miss what God has for you by taking matters into your own hand. Keep waiting on God. He will **never** forsake you nor by any means **fail** you. Wait on Him! If you say, "Lord I believe your word" then, trust Him to perform it. He will surely do it. *Make sure you remain in condition to receive it*. It can be disappointing to pray to God concerning the thorn in your flesh per se, and realize that it hasn't been removed. It can really hurt to work, hope and pray for something like a house, job, healing or promotion and not get it. Keep in mind that as much as you may desire a thing, God knows what's best for you and it is His desire to bless you. God didn't send His son to die for us without the intent of good for us. There would be no need to send His only begotten, well beloved son to give His life if God's intent was to do us harm. It was love that compelled Him to redeem us. He didn't spare His own son but He delivered him up for us all, how shall He not, with Him freely give us all things (Romans 8:32)? However, we mustn't set our thoughts on the 'things' that are freely given to us but rather on Him who freely gives. So, in whatever position you find yourself in, hold on to your faith in God and His word; even when you feel as if you are doing it alone.

Chapter 6

Walking Alone

There are times when it seems that you are all alone. During those times, God is right there even when it doesn't feel like it. Being or feeling alone at times doesn't mean that we can't enjoy the particular stage of life that we are in.

Loneliness can affect a person at any stage of life. It is common for women to feel alone during certain landmark occasions of life such as: giving birth, loss of a loved one, having children grow up and leave home, menopause and entering the golden years of life. Loneliness is also prevalent among women during years of singleness, living in a bad or abusive relationship(s), after experiencing a divorce or while coping with sickness and pain. In addition, work related loneliness is commonplace for women in the military and those who travel for a living, while many young girls face loneliness as they enter adolescence and adapt to new schools and the constant changes that are taking place in their bodies. Then, there are countless elderly women who struggle with loneliness after having to leave their homes and possessions to enter long term care facilities.

There are numerous causes of loneliness and it is fairly common among *all* of mankind. However, knowing that loneliness is common doesn't take away the negative emotions that come with it; that's something we have to personally overcome through prayer, persistence and service. That's right; loneliness is one of those things that we must actually take some action in order to overcome it.

First of all, we must come to the understanding that it is God's will that we are connected to one another. God designed us so that we are interdependent, that we have need of each other. We all need encouragement, admonition, love and edification. These are all services that we are to extend to each other. In the body of Christ; it is imperative that we stay connected in fellowship with each other. It is a necessity so that we all grow in the unity of the faith and knowledge of Jesus Christ in full measure. We are to be joined together so that every joint (person) uses the abilities and gifts that God has given him/her to supply to others, so that we may all flourish until the whole body is edified and grown in love (Ephesians 4:16). Sadly, there are many people who desperately need these services even though they are members of and/or connected to the Body of Christ. So, what do you do when you need the company and outreach of another human? First, look up before looking out. We must be sure that in everything, even when it comes to companionship, that we acknowledge God. We are not to be anxious about anything, but in everything, with prayer and supplication, we must make our request known to Him and the peace of God which passes all understanding will keep our hearts and minds (Philippians 4: 6-7).

Experiencing loneliness doesn't mean that we have to be without the peace of God that He has freely given us. After all, we were made for companionship. It is perfectly normal to desire companionship. God himself said, "It is not good for man to be alone." Then He provided the very first human companion; Woman.

Nobody—man or woman, boy or girl—really wants to be or feel alone. The feelings of loneliness can seem overpowering some days. You may find yourself sitting alone and wondering where to go or who to call and as you think, your list narrows down little by little as you realize that others are busy, unconcerned or otherwise unavailable.

Remember that Jesus is always there, He's concerned, never too busy and always available. When we cry out to Him He is able to lift our burdens, give us strength, console us and help us to move forward. Taking time to talk to God can take our minds off of ourselves and the feelings of loneliness. Then, somehow, someone reaches out with a kind word, a word in season that reminds us that we are never alone. This may be a stranger, a family member, a friend, a teacher, fellow Christian or co-worker etc. Regardless of who the person is, it's uplifting to know that God hears us. He can touch the heart of any person and put the words that we need into the mouth of another person at just the right time. Proverbs 25:11 tells us that, a word fitly spoken is like apples of gold in pictures of silver.

How precious are the right words spoken at the right time! They are priceless!

Many times our hugs, handshakes and even a smile are just what someone needed. It's true that when we give *it* shall be given unto us. The principles of giving do not apply only to money or any material gift. We must also extend service to others, knowing that these services will be extended to us, even if it's not by the same people. God is not limited to the people with whom we are daily acquainted or even to those that we know. He is able to speak to whomever He wishes in order to bless you. Therefore, we have no need or right to expect anything in return from those whom we reach out to with good deeds. Nor should we feel hurt or offended when it seems that a kindness has not been returned to us. We can be confident in God's word knowing that as we water or pour out of ourselves to others by rendering services of love, God will pour back into us. Yes, God cares so much for us that he's even concerned when we are lonely. Thank God that His resources are without limit. There is nothing that we have need of that he isn't able to supply. This includes companionship.

Oftentimes, we feel alone and we aren't really alone. We know that God is always there but many times there are also people whom we haven't considered. The fellowship we are seeking is many times right in our own surroundings such as: our church, school or workplace—but we just haven't taken the time to get acquainted. We often overlook people and opportunities that we have every day for fellowship with others and to allow them to enjoy fellowship with us. We must persistently overcome the fears of interacting with others.

There are many reasons why one might have for refraining from personal interaction in some places, and the woman who has suffered from pain and rejection in prior relationships may use seclusion as a defense mechanism. She may have deduced that the pain of loneliness is more bearable than the disappointment of another failed relationship/friendship. The idea of staying away seems easier than interacting but, it is true that in order to have friends you must first show yourself friendly. The first step to overcoming fear in this area is recognizing it. The next is to purposely extend yourself to others to make new acquaintances. It is possible to reach out to others and guard your heart at the same time. We shouldn't be pushy but we must be persistent and reach out purposefully to open lines of communication with others. Lastly, reconnect with old friends and family.

Communication is how we develop most relationships in our lives. Prayerfully reaching out to others around you through conversation is a way to connect to others. You can guard your heart by refraining from giving too much information about yourself before developing a true friendship which consists of confidentiality. Being too open too soon opens the door of your heart to the possibility of being broken if the person betrays your confidence.

Do not let the desire for intimacy trigger you to bear your soul to someone who is neither willing nor able to accept all that you are, think and feel. Not every person that enters your life will be able to connect with you on the deepest level of the core of your being. Leave that to God . . . He knows you well; there is nothing hidden from Him and He loves you despite any flaws you may have. A person who isn't able to walk in the unconditional love of God may change his or her opinion of you at the hearing of some of your thoughts and actions. God will never change his opinion of you. So, save all of your intimate details and thoughts about life for God until He places people in your life that can be trusted with them.

The word of God urges us to reach out to each other; to encourage each other on a daily basis. That is how highly God has esteemed the importance of relationships. Jesus said, "Love one another as I have loved you. By this, all men will know that you are my disciples." God takes pleasure in his children caring for one another and attending to each other's needs. We can dispel our own loneliness by dissipating someone else's loneliness.

Behold how good and pleasant it is for brethren to dwell together in unity (Psalm 133:1)!

In addition to having people in our lives that we haven't considered, we regularly have people in our lives that we have counted out. In a perfect world, family and friends would always get along and there would never be any division or disagreements. For the present time, we do not live in a perfect world. We live in a world where we must learn forgiveness and reconciliation if we want to maintain healthy relationships. Too often, family members become at odds with each other over some kind of disagreement or another. This often leads to a temporary loss of communication. In some cases, the lack of communication lingers on for years.

It is sad to think that two siblings who were raised together in the same house with the same parents can have such a falling out that they refuse to even speak to each other for several years. That is what happened to Meagan and Martha, listen to their story:

Many years ago in Iowa, two sisters we will call Meagan and Martha had a disagreement. For some reason, they didn't resolve the issue. They are presently both elderly and living in the same place. They do not speak to each other at all. Neither of them remembers exactly what happened but they both consider each other a hopeless case in respect to reconciliation. Needless to say, they both face loneliness and boredom in their present lives but refuse to forgive. They could each benefit from the company of the other if they would only forebear each other in love and look over whatever shortcomings they may think the other person has. They have already accomplished one half (forgetting) of the old phrase forgive and forget. If they would both decide to commit to the other half of the phrase (forgiveness), healing would commence and joy would prevail!

Are there people in your life whom you have discounted due to a disagreement? Do you have family and friends with whom you no longer speak to? I do realize that there are some situations that require special conditions such as cases of abuse of any form but with God, we can forgive each other, treat each other civilly, and have sincere love and concern for each other. If we focus on how we feel we have been offended, we will not forgive. If we have to contend about who is right and who is wrong, forgiveness will be hindered but when we seek to make amends, our situation becomes conducive for forgiveness. Choose to forgive and when it is possible, fellowship with family and friends who you may have been at odds with in the past. Continue to guard your heart but remember that God is glorified when we allow the love of God to overcome offenses. God is in favor of reconciliation. My dad and I can testify to the fact that God can restore relationships that have been lying dormant for years.

Read what happened for us:

When I was nineteen years old, I received a phone call from my dad. He asked if I was free to go out and have dinner together. I said, "Yes." I was very happy. My dad and I met at a restaurant in Washington, Georgia. We ate and talked for a long time. I needed that. He apologized for not being present in my life during my childhood. I could feel his sincerity. I needed my dad at that time as much as I did as a child. I forgave him.

He also noted that he had committed his life to God. I could tell that he was different just by the conversation we were having. From that day until the present time, my dad and I remain in contact with each other. I can depend on him to be there for me in whatever magnitude I need him to be. We laugh, we talk . . . . we love each other. Years ago, I counted my dad out. I didn't think we would have a real father/daughter relationship. Thank God, He never counts anyone out. I'm so grateful to my Heavenly Father for restoring my relationship with my earthly father.

God can do the same for you. He can restore a relationship that has been in ruins for years. As we choose to forgive and initiate reconciliation, God will surly bless it. Why should we walk alone when we can allow God to repair broken relationships in our lives?

At any rate, loneliness does not have to be a constant state of being, it can become momentary and those moments will get shorter and shorter through prayer to God, servicing others and persistently seeking out and being a companion to those around us. We were not made to be alone, we were made for companionship and not only that, we were made to love and be loved.

Everybody wants to be loved!

Chapter 7

Wanting to be loved

It is perfectly normal for every human to desire to be loved. It is also perfectly normal for a woman to desire to be loved by a man. We were made for the man. Therefore, it's not strange or wrong for a woman to desire to be loved by a man. In some settings women - especially Christian women - are dissuaded to desire to be married. In other settings the desire for male companionship is considered lust and something that the woman needs to be delivered from. Many women have given in to the belief that they just don't need a man while others feel guilty because they want one. However, that desire can lead to making wrong decisions when it isn't kept in the proper perspective. Denying that one desires to be married isn't the proper perspective either. Both of these methods have proven to simply cause a woman to become a target for those who are not serious about marriage but are intrigued by conquests. The last thing that a broken woman needs is to assume the role of a perpetual victim. Notwithstanding, this is often the case but, it doesn't have to be. God's grace is sufficient even for the broken and wounded. He is able to cause us to triumph, not only the strong but all those that put their trust in him. You may be thinking, "I trust God so, why does it seem that I'm continuously victimized?" First of all you must look at your circumstances and evaluate your own actions. Then, ask yourself, "Am I walking in the wisdom of God's word?"

As I reflected on my own life I realized that there were many points of brokenness in my life that resulted from not guarding my heart as the scripture says that we should. I also had to admit that there were times that I was not obedient to God or those He sent to instill wisdom into me. I know that there were things in my past that had a great impact on my decision making but I also had access to the one whom is all knowing and able to make even the simple wise. It is also an observation of psychologist that oddly enough some victims even look for approval or acceptance from their victimizers. This is why a woman who has been sexually abused may want an explanation from her predator or even blame herself. However, a predator never has compassion for its prey. It is that very nature that enables one to become such. Although forgiveness can be a hard process, it is a blessing to us that it does not require participation from both parties. There are some people who will never say I'm sorry. There are some people who will never admit a wrong doing even after seeing the effects of their actions in the lives of the other person.

The trespasses we make against ourselves and our own bodies, we must take responsibility for and receive the healing and forgiveness that God has made available to us through Jesus. When we look outside of God to find what we need there is always a risk that the perfectly normal desire to be loved can be perverted and misplaced. Many women, young and old compromise a chance for receiving true love which is patient, kind and unfailing for the feelings of love that are exchanged through sex. The problem is, those chemical exchanges that take place during intimacy are gone after the act is over and then in many cases all you are left with is someone who does not value anything about you other than physical attraction.

Sexual immorality is an enemy to all ensnared by it but it can be an emotional train wreck for a broken woman.

Momentary gratification is never worth the tradeoff of a consistent life of peace. Sexual temptations of the flesh are normally seen as a male thing. For some reason there is the impression that women who engage in pre-marital or extra-marital affairs do it for love, money, to please the man or to secure a relationship. I think maybe that makes us seem a little more prim and proper than our male counterparts if sexual contact is just a means to and end and not based upon pure gratification. Actually, most women fall into temptation because they are carried away with their own lust and overcome by it. The desire for a man is normal but fulfilling that desire outside of God's boundaries is something that must be resisted.

When a woman is plagued by the temptations of the flesh she oftentimes does not consider the blessing of peace and stability in her life because she can feel the urges of the flesh. Whenever a person greatly desires something and suffers lack in that area, focusing on that lack will diminish the awareness of the many blessings that are already in the person's possession. If we succumb to the urges of the flesh, and peace and stability are no longer abiding with us, it is then that we realize that blessed is he who endures temptation.

Needless to say moving too soon can be more costly than any kind of reward it may bring. Marriage is good and honorable in all and it is ordained by God. However, another thing that a broken women doesn't need, is to get married to someone who doesn't truly love her. The loneliness that is felt during singleness cannot be compared with the gross loneliness that comes from abuse and abandonment in a marriage. This was certainly my case.

Even now it is hard to talk about because in my heart I feel it to be my biggest failure and nothing in my life has ever caused me to feel more foolish. Many single women have felt the reproach of being saved and single. These women can relate to the feelings of inadequacy felt about questions like, "When are *you* going to get married?" Not to mention being approached by married men and men with ill intents because they consider you vulnerable because you are unattached. This is not only tiring but it feels degrading and increases the desire to be married, to be protected.

I married a man I'd never seen before in person who lived on a different continent who claimed to be a Pastor. Welcome to the global network! In the foolishness of my thinking, this was ideal. I would marry a Man of God with whom I would co-labor with in ministry and there would be no dating and no tricks. The funny thing is all I got was tricks and two beautiful little girls. To understand the story completely, I must tell it from the beginning although it may seem to you that I must have been the most stupid and naïve person on earth. Trust me there were many days I felt exactly that. But, the truth is anyone can be deceived. Deception has nothing to do with intelligence but the mindset of the deceiver and the one who is being deceived.

In December 2005, as I sat writing a psychology paper for a final exam, I was contacted by someone on yahoo messenger who claimed to be living on a refugee camp. He said he had lost his parents in the war in Liberia. He said that he was in Ghana in an internet chat room but he lived here and there finding what he could to eat and mostly sleeping at a church on the camp. He said he was 15 years old. He also added that the people who owned the internet café' would often allow displaced children like himself to use the internet in order to solicit help. Well, I had two children of my own so I googled the name of the camp of which he said he lived and read about the war. My heart was broken by the things I read and the images that I saw. I didn't know how I could have missed seeing all that had happened there on the news. However, at that time I didn't use the computer very much for anything other than school and chatting with a very few friends and family members who lived out of town. I wasn't a member of Facebook or MySpace at that time. I was not familiar with reports of internet scamming, though I'd briefly heard of it. I agreed to help him—it was not uncommon for me—if I was able, to try to help anyone who asked me. Afterwards, he sent me a message saying that he told the Pastor of the church, where he often slept, about my helping him and the Pastor wanted to meet me and invite my church ministerial team to come preach at the church on the camp. So, I communicated with the alleged Pastor on the internet mostly about the camp and the church. He told me how the church helped many of the orphaned kids there as much as they could as well as widows.

I was very interested in preaching on the camp and going to Africa. Going to Africa and preaching the gospel internationally was something that had been spoken both to and concerning me by my Pastor after I preached my second sermon. However, at the time I couldn't even imagine such a thing or how it would happen. Yet, I had a strong desire to spread the gospel and intercede for all people.

As I began to consider this opportunity, I also began to communicate regularly with this Pastor by internet and phone. Not only did I travel there in 2006 along with another minister but I also agreed to marry someone I'd never seen in person.

Right now I know you are probably thinking, "How could you be so foolish?" I too have asked myself that. During that time not only did I pray concerning this but I also fasted and I felt it was God's will. The following seven years proved to be the loneliest, most painful years of my life.

Undoubtedly, the man I married had a different purpose in mind than I had. His sole objective was to come to the US. Two months after arriving, he simply left without saying a word. I was not only distraught, I was pregnant and distraught. Twelve weeks into the pregnancy, I miscarried. I wish I could say that after this wisdom and better judgment prevailed and that I picked up the pieces and moved on by the grace of God only looking back to heal and move forward. Not so. I reconciled with him. I left my home town, my church, my family and closed my business all to move 20 hours away to the state of Minnesota with the hope of repairing and rebuilding a marriage that God could be glorified in. After all, I knew that marriage was honorable in God's sight and He takes it seriously even if we do not. I did not want to divorce again even though I knew that he was capable of just walking away and abandoning me. I also knew that our marriage would require more work than the usual hard work of any marriage and I wanted to be sure that we both gave it a genuine effort. Again, I prayed concerning it and felt I should go. Eight months later, I was pregnant again and we were both excited. Having children was very important to him. Nevertheless, five months into the pregnancy, he left the country and didn't return until our daughter was two months old. So, there I was, a woman of God, in an unfamiliar place alone having a baby without a husband or one single visitor.

Yet, even when I wanted to feel nothing but disdain and loathing for him, God's word would compel me to fill my heart with forgiveness and sorrow towards him. Regardless of how much someone may hurt us, it doesn't negate God's love for them or his perfect will, that none should perish. In his favor is always life. When our broken hearts are tempted to seek retribution, God's heart is seeking repentance. We reconciled again which produced another daughter who would not see her father in person until ten days before her first birthday.

Oddly enough, I still sensed the need to be still, be kind, be merciful and trust God. This wasn't easy and it sure didn't seem fair but then again, fair would have been for me to pay for my own sins rather than God sending his only son to do it for me. We often think that if we are devoted to God we should never suffer or be mistreated, disrespected or overlooked. We feel that we should not have to endure mistreatment; after all, we are children of the King. We tend to forget that Jesus, the only begotten son was mistreated and suffered affliction although He was faultless. So, who are we that we should be exempted from it. Still, God was working on me and developing fruits of the spirit in me. After spending months on end alone, one infidelity after another and endless displays of disrespect, through prayer and patience I finally reached a point of release. All along I hoped and prayed that my marriage regardless of its dysfunction would be healed and become a testimony. It did but, not in the way I had hoped. My husband finally said he was leaving for good. God was faithful and gave me peace and the power to forgive. By the grace of God, all was forgiven from my standpoint. I harbor no ill-will towards him in my heart and I'm grateful for our two daughters although I never intended to be a single parent again. I can't say that I have no regrets. It was hard not to wonder what my life would be like if I had made a different decision, if I hadn't helped the person who claimed to be an orphan of war. Those kinds of what ifs are the very things we can't afford to ponder on. So, I decisively chose to think on God's goodness and His word. I purposely focused on the spiritual benefits I received. This period of my life, though it was tedious, taught me a lot about myself, unconditional love and God's love and faithfulness towards us. It was during this time that God showed me things about myself that needed to be changed. It was during this time of seclusion that I was made certain that I am loved and I always have been.

Now, making wrong choices and foolish decisions are not something that anyone should be proud of. There is no glory in poor judgment nor is it glorious to continuously make mistakes. But, God is glorious and **He** can be glorified in the worst case scenario in your life. Whatever state your life is presently in, regardless of how it got in that state, God can be glorified in it. If you need salvation, He can save you. If you need deliverance, He can deliver you. If you need forgiveness, He can forgive you. If you need another chance, He can give you another chance. If you need love, He *is* love.

The longing to be loved isn't a problem as long as you are certain that you are already fully and completely loved by God. It is that very love that is life-changing and all sufficient and nothing else is capable of taking its place. If you are single and you desire to be married, there isn't a thing wrong with that. It is okay to want to be loved. But, know that though marriage is good, it will not heal an already broken spirit; only God can do that.

While you are being prepared and waiting for the right spouse, don't worry about what other people are saying. It is more important to monitor what you say.

Chapter 8

What do YOU say?

And the tongue is a fire, a world of iniquity: so is the tongue among our members, that it defiles the whole body, and sets on fire the course of nature; and it is set on fire of hell (James 3:6).

The tongue may be small but it plays a big part in the direction of our lives and our emotional state of being. We have discussed the fact that words can injure a person deeply. This also applies to the very words spoken about oneself and the issues of life. We all have opinions. Magazines and talk shows with special guest of psychologists, psycho analyst and experts of all sorts have opinions of what should be done to have a good life but, what do YOU say? God's word says, "What man is he that loves life and desires many days that he may see good. Keep your tongue from evil and your lips from deceit. Depart from evil and do good. Seek peace and pursue it" (Psalms 34:12-14). So, according to the creator of the tongue, we must be careful with its use if we want to have a good life.

Positive or rather Godly thinking and speaking isn't a suggestion for healing and deliverance of the broken woman, it is a must. Negative words can only add injury to a broken life. When I say negative words I mean words that are not consistent with God's words concerning who we are, what we are, what we can do, what we should have, how we should be and our purpose in the earth.

For instance, every time a feeling of inadequacy arises and the words 'I can't' flow from the mouth, this is inconsistent with the word of God which says I can do all things through Christ who strengthens me (Philippians 4:13). When we are plagued by thoughts of worthlessness and worry about our daily provisions, we know that God takes care of the sparrow and is concerned when one falls to the ground and we are worth far more than sparrows. We are so valuable to Him that He sent His son to die for us. Even the very hairs on our heads are numbered. Our feelings must not be allowed to override our faith or the word of God which is the basis of our confidence. Therefore, our words must not be a reflection of negative emotions nor should we allow the negative words spoken by others to control our emotions and establish our thoughts and words. For example:

An intelligent and well-spoken Woman once told me, "I just feel so unnecessary," this was the result of years of being told by her mother that she was just not going to amount to anything. She was very hard working and persistent but she faced many failures because of the negative way of thinking she had become accustomed to over the years. Regardless of her abilities or accomplishments she always felt that she wasn't adequate enough. She couldn't see the beauty that others saw in her. In addition to being highly intelligent, she was very friendly and kind to others. The negative words that were etched into her mind would not allow room for the positive words spoken concerning her by others. The old saying, "sticks and stones may break my bones but words can never hurt," is so far from the truth.

Many times words do far more damage than we think and that damage can take longer to heal, especially when they are heard over and over.

It seemed that she would never reach her goals and most of the time things turned out just the way she expected them to because she unintentionally began to believe that nothing would ever work out for her. So, even when normal everyday life inconveniences would happen to her like a disagreement with a friend or a conflict at work, she would always account it as proof that the voice in her head was correct. Before long, those thoughts were not just words her mother had spoken to her but they became her very own thoughts and began producing more and more loss of self-worth.

Thank God that even if someone else has shaped your thoughts about yourself, He is still able to work in and through you to bring about healing. God gave us a tongue and we can use it for good or bad. If you think you have no "say so" over your life, think again. You have the power to change your mind with your own tongue by speaking the word of God over yourself. When the mind is changed; the actions will follow.

Trusting God to heal brokenness goes hand and hand with keeping the right perspective- regardless of what is seen, heard or felt- and speaking words that are in alignment with God's opinion, the only opinion that is absolute truth. Jesus spoke to His disciples and said, "And you shall know the truth and the truth shall make you free" (John 8:32). We can find the truth about whom we are and the value that God has placed upon us in His word. Once we know what God says about us, what should we say about ourselves? Our words should be the same as His even if we feel defeated, His word says that, in all things we are more than conquerors through Christ Jesus who loved us and gave himself for us. When the temptation comes to accept a down trodden life as being God's intention for you remember that his truth says that we were created for good works. If you've made many mistakes that have taken you far from the path that God has intended and suffered severe damage as a result, God is still able to work in your life. As God spoke to His people in the book of Jeremiah after they had sinned, turned away from Him, and were carried off to Babylon, "For I know the thoughts I have towards you, thoughts of good and not evil to give you an expected end" (Jeremiah 29:11). God promised them that He would perform His good word towards them after their captivity was over although they had turned away from Him. He told them when they sought Him with all their hearts they would indeed find Him. Oh what a blessing! Have we not a better covenant now than they did then through the blood of Jesus? God still wants us to seek and when we do, we shall find. It is the Father's good pleasure to give us the kingdom! He will never leave us nor forsake us nor will he deny the work of His hands.

Before the world was framed, He fashioned us for His own purpose and there is nothing that can happen, will happen or has happened that surprises Him. God's word concerning those that love Him has already gone out and it will perform that which it was sent out to do. It is our responsibility to agree with it, take heed to it, declare it and walk according to it.

During especially difficult times, it can be challenging to speak positive, God-centered words over your situation. However, it is during those times that one must be specifically persistent to avoid speaking negative words. For instance, when the circumstances of your life are not good, it doesn't help to continuously speak about how bad things are. It doesn't even feel natural to say, "Things are getting better," when they appear to be getting worse. But, we are not simply natural beings, we are also spiritual beings and God has given us the authority to call those things that are not as though they were. Isn't that amazing! God has given human beings, you and I, the power to speak things into existence.

Several years ago, I attended the same church as a beautiful and talented young woman who was also single. She was the praise and worship leader and very active in the church's singles ministry. We will call her Alana. Her story sounds incredible but it is true.

Alana was not dating anyone but she would often say that she would be getting married soon. Now, this was a contrast to others who said things like, "It doesn't look like I will ever get married." Nevertheless, we would all laugh about Alana's proclamation and take it for a joke. Sometimes we would tease her and say, "To whom?" or "You need a groom first." Well, to our surprise it wasn't long at all before she met and married her partner for life. She said, "I kept telling you guys I would get married soon."

She chose to speak life to change her situation.

Today, Alana's husband is a powerful preacher of the gospel who loves her dearly. He and Alana continue to minister to God's people through song and the Word of God.

Our words **can** produce life and bring forth any good thing that is in alignment with God's will!

Let God's word be the authority over your life. Let your voice be the loudest voice to proclaim His word over your life. Allow God's word to drown out every negative thought, every negative word that attempts to take residence in your mind. Practice speaking kindly to yourself!

Here are some examples of scripturally inspired words that reign true for every believer. Allow these words to become thoughts:

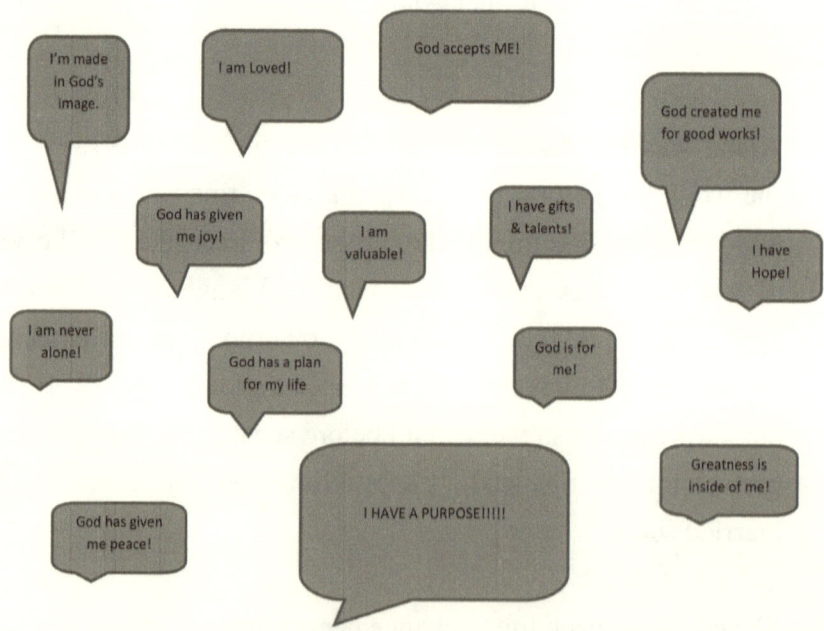

Our kind words of biblical truths must not stop with ourselves.

The words we speak concerning ourselves are very important but so are the words we speak about others as well as the attitude of the heart that is revealed in our words. Therefore, gossiping, lying, murmuring and complaining are our enemies and offenses of the tongue.

The damage that one can do to self with negative words is comparable to the damage of gossip. Even if the person that is being gossiped about never hears what was said, their character is damaged by words spoken about them that they have no way of defending. Gossip does not promote the love of God. Instead, it brings about disharmony in churches, in families, among friends, in neighborhoods and communities, on school yards and in private facilities. Gossip is never productive in any setting. There is not any good thing about it and it does not produce any good thing. The appeal of gossip is to know some secret thing but how much of a thrill is it to know some secret that isn't 100% fact. In rare cases, where gossip is actually true, put yourself in the shoes of the person who is the object of the gossip and ask yourself if you would want people passing around that kind of information about you: especially people with whom you have placed your trust.

It is astounding how we can quickly change our minds about the 'rightness' of something when it affects us. If you are thinking, "I don't like to gossip but people are always telling me something." A disapproving look on your face will turn away gossip. It is neither kind nor wise to gossip about other people. This has contributed to the brokenness of many dolls young and old. Some people put a lot of confidence in gossip and develop opinions of others based upon the gossip they've heard. This often leads to other wrong and displeasing behaviors such as lying.

When you receive gossip about someone else and it's not true, as you pass it on, you become a partaker and spreader of lies. Not that lying needs gossip to be a front man for it. No, lying is serious all on it's on. Satan is recorded as being the Father of lies. We don't need to possess any of Satan's characteristics. Jesus said, "I am the truth and the life . . ." so we should follow the way of our Lord by being truthful. When we lie, or intentionally say things that are not true, make promises that we do not intend to keep or give a false witness, it generally produces problems and it ruins our credibility. Everybody benefits when we are honest with each other!

Oftentimes, people lie when being asked questions about things they don't want to share. To avoid getting into an area they don't want to be in, they just say something. This can be avoided. I've learned that it is perfectly okay to say that's personal or I don't want to discuss that. It is well within your rights to share what you want to share or withhold what you want to withhold concerning yourself or your family. Refuse to feel cornered into lying. The same thing goes for feeling pressured to give a yes or no to an invitation when you know you are not sure. Let the person know that you have other things pending. Tell them you aren't sure yet and you don't want to give a yes or no answer.

Lying is very injurious to one's character. We have all lied but some people, especially those who want to discredit you will hold onto something you said that wasn't true for years and then use it as a measurement for everything else you say. It is also dishonest to try to provoke someone else to lie by asking questions to "see what the person will say." Honesty is really the best policy! It pleases God and it is constructive for us.

Honesty is imperative when receiving emotional healing. Holding back or watering down circumstances will only prohibit restoration. We must be honest with ourselves and about ourselves. It is not always easy to come to terms with our own faults but they too must be faced in order to heal. As with anything else, honesty is a choice. We must choose to speak the truth and avoid murmuring and complaining.

When we murmur and complain about things, it seems harmless but everything we do is an act of faith or an act of doubt. When we murmur it projects discontentment, ungratefulness and doubt. Why should we complain if we know that God is in control and **He** knows what **He** is doing? Why should we murmur when we have access to God through prayer? Through Christ, we have a relationship with God and therefore we have no reason to murmur when we can simply talk to God freely. Any parent can tell you that it is frustrating to be driving to a restaurant to have dinner and hear a child murmuring and whining on the back seat who is old enough and capable of talking. It is even more frustrating when the parent asks what's wrong only to hear, 'I'm hungry." The parent responds, "We're going out to eat, we're almost there." The murmuring is so unnecessary. It is the same way with us. God knows where we are, He knows our circumstances and He is working on our behalf. We don't know His schedule. Oftentimes we are almost there (where God is trying to take us) when we show our doubt through murmuring.

Complaining is the twin sister of murmuring. To always have a problem with this or that is a sign of ungratefulness. We must be careful to resist the temptation to protest and criticize the people, things and conditions in our life. Complaining is a waste of words. It does not repair or change anything. Contentment is the remedy for complaining. The ability to be grateful for the state we are in is incalculable. Godliness with contentment is great gain! (I Timothy 6:6)

I wish I had known that complaining doesn't help anything years ago when I was waiting for my aunt to repair my broken doll. I was anything but content. Every time I wanted to play with the doll and she was not ready, I would start complaining about the fact that she was torn in the first place. The doll was torn by mistake and I knew that but the fact that I didn't have her to play with caused me to look around to cast blame. I guess, all in all, I just wanted her back so she could serve the purpose for which she was given to me.

Chapter 9

Misplaced Purpose

My doll was a gift, her purpose was to be a companion and bring me enjoyment. When she was broken, I could no longer enjoy her because I could see her brokenness and I just wanted her to be the same as she had been. I was afraid to handle her because I didn't want to cause further damage. She didn't function or appear to be the valuable doll I'd received. Likewise, when a woman is broken, she just wants to be fixed. Her actions and appearance often reflect her inward brokenness and she lives in fear of accumulating more damage. The result is an inability to walk in the purpose for which she was created.

Brokenness can cause a woman's value to be reduced in her own eyes; this can lead to a misplaced purpose. When a woman's value is lost or rather misplaced, it can lead to all kinds of degrading behavior and acceptance of degradation from others. That's why a broken woman may voluntarily put up with abuse and actually believe she deserves it or that it's better than having nothing at all. It seems that when you are broken, abuse and failure attempt to become a natural part of life and inevitably an expected part of life. This can lead to more poor choices which accumulate additional negative consequences. Therefore, fulfilling the idea that life will always be this way. It's true that the spirit of a man sustains him in infirmity but who can bear a broken spirit (Proverbs 18:14)? The answer is no one; a broken spirit breeds depression and negativity which often leads to attachment of labels and stigmas that are hard to overcome alone. It is hard for a woman to see any purpose of good for her life when she is in this state. It is hard to even conceive of the fact of divine purpose in ones broken and shattered life. However, in the midst of wanting and needing to be healed, God's purpose for her life in His master plan and in the lives of others doesn't change.

What is your purpose? If you've ever known, it hasn't changed. Just as nothing can change the love of God for you, nothing can change the purpose for which you were made. God is not a man that He should lie, neither the son of man that He should repent. Has He said it, shall He not do it has He spoke it, shall He not make it good (Numbers 23: 19). We were created for good works that our lives may be beneficial to us and others. We did not earn salvation nor have we earned the purpose that God has given us. In all of His divine wisdom He chose you for a specific purpose and He has given you all that you need to complete that purpose. For everything that pertains onto this life and Godliness, He has given to us according to His power (II Peter 1:3). It doesn't matter what you've gone through, He still loves you and His purpose for you is the same. He who made you is able to do in and through you that which He has purposed.

Now, there's more good news. You don't even have to spend all of your days and nights thinking of yourself and how you will fulfill your purpose or how you will fix the broken areas of your life. Even with the best intentions, this can become selfishness. Your initial assignment is simply to receive the help you need that is already available to you. Jesus said, "come unto me all who labor and are heavy laden and I will give you rest" (Matthew 11:28). We can come to Him casting our cares upon Him because He cares for us. If you've ever felt like anyone cared for you, He cares more. Opening up to Jesus is the very best thing a broken woman can do for healing and recovering her purpose. He is the answer for every broken heart and seemingly hopeless situation. For by Him were all things created, that are in heaven, and that are in earth, visible and invisible, whether *they be* thrones, or dominions, or principalities, or powers: all things were created by Him, and for Him (Colossians 1:16). This includes you and I, we were made for Him and He knows exactly what we should be doing. There is no greater source of direction than from the one who made the path you are traveling.

Sitting and obsessing about your purpose and what you should be doing can cause self-centeredness which will still leave you without direction or the zeal to do the things you know you should be doing. One thing our purpose is not, is neglecting the needs of others who are our responsibility in order to find purpose. Prayer and intercession is the way to seek out your purpose without being self-seeking. Continuous thinking, analyzing and confining your prayers to be about yourself will not lead you to your purpose; it will still be misplaced. As we pray for ourselves we must not forget to intercede for others. We should not seek our own but we should seek the wealth (good) of others (I Corinthians 10:24). In doing this we cultivate love and thus fulfill one of the purposes of the Sons of God—to love our neighbors as ourselves.

Secondly, we must do the things we know we should do. Brokenness does not exempt a woman from day to day responsibilities though it may impede her. It is difficult to take care of others in the home, fulfill obligations in the work place when a person is in physical, emotional, psychological or spiritual anguish. Yet, it must be done and God is our strength in our weakest moments if we rely on Him. It is during the times that God seems so far away when He is closest to us. For, He is near to those who have a broken heart and saves those with a contrite spirit (Psalms 34:18). This may sound cliché but it is true. Regardless of how simplistic prayer and having a heartfelt conversation with God may seem during a crisis or long periods of hurt or loneliness, there is no counselor like the Wonderful Counselor. There is no greater comfort than the comfort God left for us, the Holy Spirit. Our God is able to heal and deliver, to lift up the head that was bowed down and turn you in the right direction. It's amazing what prayer can do. It is even more amazing how a personal relationship with God can bring peace to a completely disheveled life. He can also help us to take our minds off of ourselves and set it on Him.

So, where should the line be drawn? How does a woman know when she is simply giving due attention to issues in her life and the will of God for her life by showing sensible concern for herself or has become selfish?

The definition of selfishness is to be concerned excessively or exclusively with oneself: seeking or concentrating on one's own advantage, pleasure or well-being without regard for others. Becoming a selfish person is a silent temptation for every broken woman. When a woman suffers deep emotional pain it can trigger her to try to protect herself at all costs. Oftentimes she feels that she is all alone and must guard; guide and help herself. Meanwhile, this is a subtle enemy and the woman may not see herself as being selfish at all. After all, it may seem to her as though everyone she has trusted has let her down, she has been abused and now she must do what she can to make herself happy.

For instance, for several months before I received Jesus Christ as my Lord and Savior at the age of 22, I had two young children and I loved them but I was broken. I was tired of disappointments and overwhelmed by the responsibility of self-employment, single parenthood, caring for a child with special needs and my own inward struggles. I became a mother at such a young age and by the time I was twenty one, I had already been married and separated . . . I was broken all to pieces. I had no idea how to fix myself but fixing myself and trying to be happy, were the things that consumed my life. As I look back I can recall many times putting my own pleasure before my children by partying, staying out all night and leaving them with family members. It is true that every now and then everyone needs a break but there must be a balance. A break should be a short interval of rest that is not equivalent or exceeding the time spent with your minor children. I didn't know that having sensible concern for one's self such as taking care of one's mental, physical, emotional and spiritual well-being could easily cross the line of selfishness if it isn't done properly.

It is important that who or what we turn towards to heal our brokenness doesn't cause further damage such as riotous living and ungodly behavior. To give attention to vain desires and give them precedence in our lives in order to heal our hurts is pure selfishness not to mention damaging.

In families, brokenness often spreads in a household because one or both parents thinks more highly of themselves, their ambitions and their happiness than the happiness and security of the family. For this cause one of every three children in America is growing up in a home with an absent father. This leaves a lot of responsibility for single moms and it makes sensible self-concern mandatory and leaves no room for selfishness. Selfishness ruins relationships but sensible self-concern should improve us and our relationships. In order to become the opposite of selfish which is selfless, we must be made whole. This is especially important for mothers who have suffered abuse and more so single mothers who are doing a lot and doing it alone.

Becoming a mother requires a great degree of selflessness because you have instantly gained someone who is completely dependent upon his/her parents to meet every need. Unfortunately, the children do not wait to grow or have needs until its mother has recovered from bad experiences, abuse or childhood pains.

All of the child's needs are immediate. For the mother, selflessness must be a choice as much as seeking help for healing. This can be difficult for a broken woman especially if she regards needing or asking for help as a failure. Remember, she's always trying to avoid any further pain. Nevertheless, when you become aware of issues that need to be addressed within yourself in any area, it is not only sensible self-concern but when you realize the affect that these things could have on your children, it can also become an act of selflessness to override the feelings of pride, fear and shame to receive what is needed to become a better you in order to become a better mother, wife, friend, sister etc.

Women are capable of doing anything but God never intended for us to be obliged or **have** to do everything. We were created to help. Helping requires selflessness, the ability to put the needs of something or someone before your own. Unfortunately, we do not live in an ideal world. Many women **<u>must</u>** do it all. In such cases, God is able to give the grace to do what needs to be done and the ability to do it well. He is also able to provide people and organizations to help us when we need it.

God is orderly and if we hope to walk in the purpose for which we were made we have to have order in our lives and make God's will a priority.

Which brings us to the third point, after seeking God and doing the things we know we should do; we must extend ourselves to Godly service. As we do this, we will start to realize our areas of strength and recognize what we naturally enjoy doing that is beneficial to the Kingdom of God. There is nothing more rewarding and fulfilling than grasping our divine purpose even if we have some failures along the way. By the grace of God, we know that he orders the steps of the righteous and as we trust God, He will direct us to our destiny.

Trusting in God can turn what seems to be an inescapable failure into a success. But, **we must put our faith in him and him alone!**

Chapter10

Have Faith in God!

Placing our confidence in God signifies our knowledge of His love for us and it displays our reliance upon Him. It is absolutely impossible to please God without faith. It is the same kind of reliance that a small child has towards a loving parent. It's no wonder that Jesus uses children as an example of faith saying, "Verily I say unto you, except ye be converted, and become as little children, ye shall not enter into the kingdom of heaven" (Matthew 18:3). He, the son of the living God had full and complete trust in his Father. So much so that whatever the Father spoke to Him, He did. We have no better example to follow than Jesus Himself. The fact that He exhibited faith in the Father and never relied on any other source indicates that we are to do the same. Jesus had all power in His hands yet, He put His confidence in the one who placed all powers in His hands.

Likewise, as we discover the many gifts, talent and abilities that we possess our reliance must be directly and exclusively in God. The wisdom of this world, success, money and power are no replacement for faith in God. Whatever we possess must be submitted to God and not used as substitutions for God. Even the very gifts and callings that God has given us are not sufficient for us to depend upon. Self-reliance is a common pitfall and a foe that we should steer clear of.

Many hurting women become self-reliant without really knowing it. Self-reliance can mask itself as a result of strength. It can *appear* to be a positive form of independence and it can be flattering to be considered a strong and independent woman. Not many women become independent by way of strength. Many women become independent through weakness after experiencing a disappointment(s). People often put confidence in people and things other than God. If we are hurt or let down by those people or things, oftentimes we undertake to rely upon ourselves to get things done, to make things happen. We think that we cannot disappoint ourselves. We know that we want what *we* believe is best for ourselves; so it's easy to rely on ourselves.

Now, there's nothing wrong with working hard, doing what needs to be done while depending upon God. The problem comes when we have unresolved issues that cause us to lack faith in God to fix the things in our lives that need to be fixed, meet our needs, or give us our heart's desire. Very few people literally say, "I don't trust you God." Yet, we show distrust by relying on ourselves to the point that we feel that we are our own greatest assets; that 'we' can bring about our own success. Here is an example:

> Corrine was a sweet and giving young lady. She was a good friend to her friends and she did whatever she could to help the members of her family. Corrine was 18 years old and she was accustomed to working hard and being successful at school and at her part time job. But she harbored many pains and disappointments from her past. You couldn't tell from looking at her, but the catalyst for all of Corrine's hard work was to escape the pain of her past. But her efforts without God's guidance only brought her past back to stare her in the face.

Corrine had become very dependent upon herself. She went to church and even prayed but she did not have faith in God that He would bring her into the kind of life that she desired. She thought that she could work hard and change the depressive outlook of her life that seemed to have been established in her childhood. Corrine's family didn't have much at all when she was growing up. Things like education weren't encouraged in her family because her mother had to focus on trying to keep food on the table. Her mother cared for Corrine, three brothers and two sisters alone. Her mother sacrificed a lot to care for her kids, and sometimes did questionable things to provide for them. Corrine didn't understand why her family seemed to struggle so much and often didn't have things they needed. The children were picked on at school and some people in their community looked down on Corrine and her family.

One day, when she was a child, Corrine overheard a conversation between two women in her community. They were talking about Corrine's family and how they pitied them. One of the women said, "Humph, them boys gon end up in jail." The other woman agreed and said, "Them girls gon be just like their mama with a house full of children with different daddies." From that moment, Corrine began to loathe herself, her mom and her family dynamics. She purposed within herself that her life would not be the way those women had said it would be. She would be different.

As Corrine grew, she worked hard to avoid the sad outcome that had been predicted. She married young, at the age of 19. Her husband was older but he was smart and accomplished. She knew her past was far behind her and she would have a good life. She and her husband had four children within seven years. When the last child was only a year old, her husband was killed in an accident. Corrine was devastated.

She remarried two years later and had two additional children. Her husband was not a man of noble character, and after five years of marriage, he deserted her for another woman. Corrine was terrified when she looked at the faces of her children; she remembered the words of the whispering women. *Corrine had made choices that she thought would take her far away from her childhood but at last, her family dynamics were the same.*

As a middle aged woman who is now content with her life, Corrine admitted that though she told God about the fears she had about her life, she never trusted that He had a good plan for her life. She recalls how she thought that she had to make her life different. She had relied on herself, her hard work and her decision making to bring about a good life. Based upon what she saw life to be as a child, she had thought that maybe her life was just meant to be a struggle and if her life was meant to be that way then that must have been the way God designed it. So, she didn't truly seek God pertaining to leading and guiding her life though, she prayed for others. She assumed that His plan for her wasn't good so, she was unconsciously and indirectly fighting against God and what *she* thought was His will for her life. Instead of turning to God who loved her and wanted to bless her she chose to depend upon herself because the hurt of her past had produced the wrong thinking that caused her to feel that God wasn't for her and that He wasn't going to help her.

In order for Corrine to finally be free, she had to commit those negative thoughts that she had concerning God's will for her to God. She also had to submit her ways, and her work to Him and ask God for His guidance. When she did earnestly pray to God concerning those things, the peace that she once appeared to have on the outside at the age of 18 was then truly present on the inside and it penetrated to the outside!

If you can relate to Corrine's story, consider this: put no confidence in the flesh, not even your own. If you've been hurt and disappointed and feel that your life is stuck in some kind of a mold that was cut out for you, a mold that you can't seem to break free of, look to God. If people look at you and see a strong independent woman but on the inside you know you are working as hard as you can and running as fast as you can to try to escape your past: Look to God and lay down those heavy burdens. Have faith in God! Bare your soul to Him and ask Him to heal you. Remember: **You do not have to rely only on yourself nor do you have to be afraid**!

However, one of the most common pitfalls for a broken woman is fear. Fear is the result of terribly misplaced faith or rather a distorted faith. Fear implies that there is a possibility of failure but faith is assured that there is no failure in God. Fear focuses on circumstantial evidence rather than the truth of God's word. Fear grows and swells according to the senses, what we see and how we feel. Nevertheless, it can bring forth results.

Just ask Abraham and Sarah (Genesis chp.18):

When they were told that Sarah, who was well past child bearing age, would bring forth a child and that the child would be Abraham's heir, as time passed, Sarah began to fear that she would not get pregnant. Sarah's womb had been closed and she had never given birth before. During those times it was shameful for a woman to not be able to give birth. Apparently, at the stage of life that Abraham and Sarah were now in, that reproach probably had passed and Sarah may have made peace with the fact that she didn't have children. Nevertheless, an Angel had spoken to Sarah saying that she would birth a child from Abraham's loins. Somehow Sarah got the idea that God would use Hagar her handmaid to birth the child. I don't know if Sarah saw herself insufficient because of her long term condition because she laughed initially when she was informed of her impending pregnancy. She had no doubt given up on the thought of child bearing. Her fear conceived and it gave birth to some very undesirable circumstances. Her age and failure to reproduce previously had become the measure of her faith in that area. Perhaps Sarah didn't want it to seem as if she was holding up the blessing that God had promised to Abraham because she didn't believe she would actually get pregnant. After all, her handmaid's child would be considered hers because the child would be her property. Regardless of whether Sarah was afraid to be disappointed or was afraid to disappoint, her fear caused her to make a decision that would bring results that were unfavorable to her and her family and all families of the earth today. Sarah had a son as the angel promised, they called him Isaac. Until this present day, the descendants of Isaac and the descendants of his brother Ishmael (Hagar's son) are still fighting.

We must not measure God's ability to perform His will in our lives by any real or perceived afflictions. Having and acting upon pessimistic thoughts concerning the present or the future based upon disappointments in the past will only bring forth the feared outcome of misplaced faith. It is through love that fear is overcome. Not merely, our love for God but because of God's love for us. Fear isn't certain of God's love therefore one who fears has not been made perfect in love meaning that the person who fears has not come into maturity of understanding God's love.

The woman who understands how much she is so greatly loved by her Father has confidence that He is on her side and though He sees her brokenness He will not exploit it but he longs to heal and bless her. She knows that when she prays her Father hears her and even if things don't go as she desires when she desires, her Father is with her every step of the way. This is that perfect love which casts out fear, love that has full assurance and all faith in the unconditional Love of God. This Love which is manifested in faith, never fails.

My mind goes back to my doll and how fond I was of her and how proud I was to have her. As I ruminated, it dawned on me that I never asked my mom to replace the doll. In the end, she was just a doll. Money was tight back then and it was not very likely that she would have been replaced. But that didn't matter because I wanted *her*. I wanted *her* to be repaired. God feels the same way about you and more so. He wants **you** and He wants **you** made whole. **You cannot be replaced.** You are more than just a doll. **You are greatly loved and you are irreplaceable!**

Chapter 11

More Than Just A Doll

My doll didn't possess any gifts or talents; she <u>was </u>a gift. She could not move, speak or feel. *She was just a doll.* She was pretty. However, she didn't have to deal with insecurities about herself or her appearance. She didn't have to be concerned with being compared to or measured by the size, looks or accomplishments of other dolls. She didn't have an agenda or plan for her life. She did whatever I planned for her. My doll had no pleasure in her existence. I enjoyed having her as my own but belonging to me had no positive effects on her at all.

In many ways today's society has reduced the status of the woman to that of "glorified dolls." A woman who isn't sure who she is can become worn out trying to meet all of society's standards for the woman. *It can be a lot of pressure trying to look just right, have the right amount of accomplishments, to think, feel and act right, make the right amount of money, do things right—to **be** just right.* If that isn't enough, women are often expected to be unaffected by the many things that can happen while you are in the midst of trying to replicate the looks of a Barbie doll and imitate the feats of a wonder woman action figure.

Like dolls, women are expected to endure whatever comes along without feeling pain.

Many women ignore their pain because they feel they should be able to just get over whatever problem they have or abuse they have suffered. Women are told to be strong and we can be, but when pain is present there must be healing. It is not socially acceptable for women to show certain emotions because it can be interpreted as a sign of weakness. But today it is much more acceptable for a woman to show anger and retaliate than to express sadness or hurt. In other settings, it is preferred that the woman be quiet and beautiful and just lie around as a doll waiting to be given some attention.

In some African cultures a woman is thought to be strong if she endures being abused and maintains her home. In many cultures submission is cloak for abuse. It is a common belief that if a woman is married and there are problems in the marriage, the woman is the one who should work to make her home happy so that the marriage can thrive. This is a misuse of scripture.

Marriage is a responsibility of both parties, but the man and the woman each have different roles. The woman is commanded to respect her husband, submit to him and guide her house well. The man is commanded to be the leader of his house, love his wife and sacrifice for her (Ephesians 5:22-27) (I Timothy 5:14). A man is not justified in adultery because his wife didn't cook dinner or because the house was not cleaned properly nor is a woman justified in adultery if her husband is inattentive or not working.

As the leader, the man is the one who God holds responsible for shaping the structure of the home. In any other setting, the leader of a thing is always responsible for initiating change or progress. The drawback with placing all of the responsibility of producing a successful marriage on the woman is that it indirectly holds her responsible for the problems in the marriage. If the woman works tirelessly to make a "happy home" and things do not work out after she has done all she can do, her self-esteem can plummet.

Here's an example:

> When Sarah and John married, they both appeared to be very happy. They lived in Philadelphia but they were both from countries in western Africa. Things were going well financially; they both had good careers and they were enjoying their new life together.

> However, Sarah's job was demanding. She had a very high salary, but she had to give a lot of time and attention to her work. John knew this before they were married and he had no problem with it. They shared all of their finances and combined they were able to live the standard of life they both wanted.

> All was well until Sarah got sick at work and came home to find John with a woman in the house. The woman was beautiful but her mannerism and appearance was a contrast to Sarah's conservative style. Sarah thought the woman was a prostitute. A confrontation ensued. Sarah learned that John had been seeing the woman before they were married and that this was not the only woman John had been with since their marriage.

> John said to Sarah, "You're my wife and these things mean nothing." He went on to explain how he'd always enjoyed the company of women. Sarah loved John and she wanted her

marriage to work. It was customary in her culture to seek help from other family members in a case such as theirs. A family council was called to discuss the matter and to promote the marriage.

Sarah and John both gave their stories about what was taking place in the marriage and what happened on the day that Sarah found John home with the woman. John made complaints about Sarah's work hours, her style of dress and her personality as a whole. These were things John had never mentioned to Sarah. John manipulated the council by saying things that were not true but were believable. For instance, Sarah and John were from different tribes, and there was a stereotype about Sarah's tribe that implied that its women were very disrespectful and rude to their men. So, when John said that Sarah did not respect him and wanted to be in charge of everything, it appeared to be true. They all knew the tribe that Sarah was from and that she made more money than John.

During the counsel it was stated that John was wrong for having the woman in the house yet, the rest of the advice and admonition was given to Sarah.

Sarah was told that she must make her home happy. The council also told Sarah that she should respect her husband, spend more time at home and less time at work. She was told that she should change the way she dressed to make herself more appealing.

Before Sarah found out about the affairs, she was a beautiful, accomplished and confidant woman who was at peace with herself and who she was. After the affair and the counsel she was given, she began to scrutinize everything about herself. Although John's first answer to her after being caught in adultery was, "I've always enjoyed the company of women;"

Sarah still felt responsible for John's actions. She felt that if she changed then, John would be faithful. She thought that if she behaved the way John wanted her to behave, if she dressed the way he wanted her to dress and was always available, then John would respect his wedding vows.

After Sarah made many changes, John remained unfaithful. Sarah was left feeling as if there must be something wrong with her. She had come to terms with the way things were but she was very unhappy.

Sarah and John went to church regularly but Sarah decided to become serious about her faith. She began to pray often. As she did this she became stronger and stronger. Her faith in God grew and the view she had adopted of herself began to change. Sarah began again dressing the way she felt comfortable, the way that fit her personal style and personality. She started to smile and laugh again.

John noticed but he didn't know what to make of it. One Saturday night while he was getting dressed to go out to a party something different happened. Sarah didn't like to party before or after they married but after the infidelity, it was one of the things she was advised to do when John wanted to go out; she should accompany him. Sarah had been reluctantly going each time John wanted to go out.

On this particular night, Sarah had told herself she would not go. She wanted to rest up for church and she had come to the conclusion that she would not babysit John. She had finally realized that his infidelity was not her fault and she would not go to the party to try to ensure his fidelity.

When John saw that Sarah was not dressed, he smiled and said, "Oh, you're not going?" Sarah looked John in his eyes and said, "No, I'm not. I married you because I loved you and I wanted to spend my life with you but you have not been faithful to the vows we made since we made them. If you want to go out to be with someone else, go, don't come back and you can take these with you." She gave him the skimpy clothes that she had bought to please him. She went on to say that they would sell the house and cut their losses.

John was baffled. He went outside and then returned back inside the house and went to bed.

The next morning John and Sarah went to church. John requested counseling from the Pastor of the church that they attended.

By the grace of God their marriage was eventually restored!

It turned out the change in Sarah that made a difference wasn't an outward change, it was an inward change. It was an inward change that came from faith in God, and knowing she was doing God's will and also that God can heal pain and give you peace with yourself. Sarah came to the conclusion that she did not have to try to become someone of value by conforming to a certain image. When she saw herself through the word of God she realized that she had *always* been valuable.

SO ARE YOU!

You are more than just a doll: your pain is real and it's okay because God can heal it. You were not created to be re-created at the propulsion of man. We can take a doll and change her clothes, give her pretend voices and different personalities, but **you** were made with a unique personality, a unique style and for a unique purpose. YOU are the best YOU there ever was or that will ever be.

You are so much more valuable than a doll. A doll's value can vary because its price range. There are dolls with very meager price tags and there are dolls that are very expensive because of who made them, the kind of doll it is or even who they had belonged to.

But women, we were carefully formed and molded from the rib of man. We were made with love and we cannot be duplicated. There is no one in the world quite like **you**. The way you laugh, the way you move, the way you speak—all of your characteristics are your very own. You are priceless. A king, **The King**, died for you and purchased an everlasting life of joy and peace just for you. Everything about you says **invaluable.**

If your value was calculated according to the fame of your designer, hands down you were created by the first and best designer there ever was or ever will be. You are an original and your creator's work can be seen everywhere, from the moon and the stars to the earth and the sea. Nobody has been able to successfully improve upon or even match his work! Whether you are married or single, you still belong to your creator, THE MOST HIGH GOD! There is nothing that can lessen or increase your value . . . . not weight gain, not weight loss, education, no education, being able to cook, not being able to cook, having good behavior, having bad behavior, being abused or being treated well, having a high powered career or taking care of the home . . . . You are Incomparable!

You are more than just a doll. Your life has a purpose that is beneficial to you and others. You were meant for more than someone else's pleasure. It is true that we were created for companionship but we were also created because we are necessary! Don't allow the ungratefulness of people to cause you to feel useless. The world would not be the same without woman. When we look at Adam and Eve it is apparent that God introduced male/ female marital relationship immediately. This is God's only structure of marriage. But not every person will marry. This fact does not lessen your value or purpose one iota.

God said, "It's not good for man to be alone, I will make a help meet for him." This is sometimes interpreted as help mate but in actuality it means what it says—a help that is meet, or necessary for him. Eve was necessary!

You are necessary!

Adam was given dominion over the earth and **so was Eve**. So even if a woman isn't married she still has the God given authority that God gave us from the beginning and the spiritual power and authority that we received in the atonement of Christ by way of the Holy Spirit.

You may feel pain, you may be alone in respects to marital status but you are neither helpless nor hopeless. You may have been discarded as a broken doll but you are not cast down and you will not be destroyed. God is able to uphold you with the right hand of his righteousness and restore you to the condition that he originally intended for you before that thing (you fill in the blank) happened to you. You can and you will make it!

I can still remember as a child, the day my aunt finished my doll and gave her back to me. She looked great but she wasn't exactly the way she was. She was repaired and you couldn't tell that she had been torn. I was glad. My aunt told me she had to make some changes because of the kind of stich that the original maker had used. Nevertheless, I was thankful and happy to have her back.

Now, as a grown Woman of God who has been healed of many hurts and emotional dysfunctions, I'm thankful for the help that I got from friends, family and counseling but I'm most grateful for the Master Craftsman! There are some "stiches" that only he can make.

There is nobody on the face of the earth, above the earth or below that earth that is like Him.

So what do we do when dolls are broken? We place them in the Master's hand and he binds up that which was broken!

You do not have a problem that is too complicated for Him. You can rely on God! When He is done with you, no one will be able to tell what your condition was before you put yourself in the Craftsman's hand. His work in you not only repairs the things about you that people can see; it also opens a door to bring out the invaluable treasures that He has placed inside of you. At that point, everyone who comes in contact with you will know that **you are more than just a doll.**

You are a Woman, You are blessed and You are a blessing!

<u>Prayer</u>

Father, touch every hurting woman who is reading this book.

Assure her of your undying love for her and give her peace.

Abba, heal every wound and bring forth the purpose for which she was created.

Those that have not been born again, draw them by your Holy Spirit and

win them with your loving kindness that they may believe in their hearts that

Jesus died for the sins of the world and you raised him

from the dead after three days in the grave.

Then, give them the boldness to

confess it with their mouths.

Father we thank you for

taking simple truths and

transforming lives.

In the name of Jesus, Amen.

Practical Tools for Repair

Often times at the end of giving an insightful sermon, my pastor will say, "Now, **so what**?" He then gives practical instructions of how to live out the message. Listed below you will find practical steps to emotional healing as well as practical points on how to heal after a rape or sexual assault.

Tips for Emotional Healing

- Acknowledge the need for healing
- Prayer (Talk to God and release your thoughts and feelings to him as you seek his guidance.)
- Seek Help (Counselor, Friend/family member, Medical Doctor, Pastor Etc.)
- Forgive (Yourself as well as anyone who has violated you)
- Get busy helping others (outreaches, relief programs, children's hospital, long term health facilities, women's shelters, mentoring programs etc.)

Healing after Sexual Assault

- Talk to someone you trust
- Identify false guilt
- Forgive yourself /forgive your perpetrator
- Identify negative ways you are responding to the attack
- Seek God and find your identity in him
- Give yourself time for renewal
- Help others

Help Lines

Family Life/Rape Recovery 1-800-358-6329

National Center on Domestic and Sexual Violence
Hotline: (800) 799-SAFE (7233) or (800) 787-3224 (TTY)
Phone: (512) 407-9020 (Administration)
Web: **http://www.ncdsv.org**

International Sexual Assault Centers
Web: **http://rainn.org/get-help/**
sexual-assault-and-rape-international-resources

U.S. National Suicide Prevention Lifeline: 1-800-273-8255
Kristin Brooks Hope Center Hope line: 1-800-784-2433

Sources

Wallenstein, Judy: *The unexpected Legacy of Divorce: A twenty five year landmark study.* (Hyperion, 2000)

www.kingjamesbibleonline.org

http://www.scientificamerican.com/article.
cfm?id=is-divorce-bad-for-children

www.apa.org/pi/families/resources/child-sexual-abuse.aspx

www.childhelp-usa.com/pages/statistics

www.familylife.com/rape/recovery

About the Author

Angela Bufford Taye

Angela is the mother of four beautiful children, Cordney, Michael, Gia and Tia. She is a born-again Christian who was licensed to minister the Word of God on December 26, 2004. Angela's agenda is to spread the love of God and the good news of the gospel wherever she goes and to be a vessel for emotional healing, deliverance and encouragement for women all over the world. It is Angela's desire to extend the love, compassion, help and hope that God has given her to other women who are in need. It is Angela's desire to fulfill the will of God for her life and to encourage others to do the same.

She has been a Licensed Master Cosmetologist for the past 19 years. Angela enjoyed many years of entrepreneurship as Owner/

Operator of Serenity I Beauty Salon before relocating to Minnesota in 2009. Angela presently works in long term health care as a Nurse Assistant where she serves and ministers to the physical, emotional and social needs of the residents

About the Book

There are two things that I'm absolutely certain of; God loves us and He is faithful. The events in this life don't always reflect God's great love and faithfulness nor do the emotions we can develop in response to the pain and disappointments of this life. This book contains life stories that are surrounded by encouragement, hope and declaration of God's unfailing love. When Dolls are Broken will assist you in seeing that God has a good and perfect will for you in the midst of and in spite of heartache, disappointment, abuse, dysfunction and depression. Regardless of your past or present state this book will inspire you to move closer to the person God created you to be.